CAMBRIDGE LATIN COURSE

A STUDENT'S LATIN GRAMMAR

by
Robin M. Griffin

Manchester Grammar School, Manchester, England

Revised & Supplemented for North American Students
by
Ed Phinney

Chair, Department of Classics & Faculty Director
University Foreign Language Resource Center
University of Massachusetts at Amherst, U.S.A.

W9-BWT-282

CAMBRIDGE
UNIVERSITY PRESS

Published by the Press Syndicate of the University of Cambridge
The Pitt Building, Trumpington Street, Cambridge CB2 1RP
40 West 20th Street, New York, NY 10011–4211, USA
10 Stamford Road, Oakleigh, Victoria 3166, Australia

First published 1992

Printed in the United States of America

Library of Congress cataloguing in publication data

Griffin, Robin M.
    A student's Latin grammar/by Robin M. Griffin; revised & supplemented for
  North American students by Ed Phinney.
        p.   cm.
    At head of title: Cambridge Latin course.
    Includes index.
    ISBN 0-521-38587-3 (pbk.)
        1. Latin language – Grammar – 1976–   I. Phinney, Ed.   II. Title.
    III. Title: Cambridge Latin course.
    PA2087.5.G75   1992   91-39825
    478.2′421 – dc20   CIP

ISBN 0 521 38587 3 paperback

Cover illustration: Wall-painting from Pompeii showing Paquius Proculus and his
wife; reproduced by courtesy of the Ancient Art and Architecture Collection.

Book design by Marcus Askwith

DS

ACKNOWLEDGEMENTS

I should like to express my warmest thanks to the many people who have helped with the writing and production of this grammar: the members of the Cambridge School Classics Project team; the Cambridge University Press editorial staff; Professor Allen and Cambridge University Press for permission to make use of the summary of recommended pronunciation in *Vox Latina* by W.S. Allen (C.U.P. 1965, 2nd edition 1978); and many others who have scrutinised draft material, made suggestions and criticisms, and been ever-ready with advice, encouragement and support. I should in particular like to thank Patricia Acres, Maire Collins, William Duggan, Vivienne Hayward, Jean Hubbard, Professor E.J. Kenney, Anne Mathews, Elizabeth Merrylees, Martin Moore, Betty Munday, Nick Munday, Pam Perkins, Professor Ed Phinney, Keith Rose, Tim Scragg, Pat Story, Alex Sutherland and David Wilson. I have gratefully adopted many of the suggestions made by those who read the grammar at draft stage; responsibility for errors and omissions is mine.

R.M. Griffin

CONTENTS

PART THREE: WORD ORDER AND SENTENCE STRUCTURE

PART FOUR: MISCELLANEOUS

STUDENT'S INTRODUCTION

This book is designed for two purposes:

1   *Reference*, i.e. for looking up a point that is causing difficulty or uncertainty. Part One ("Morphology") sets out the full system of Latin word-endings, and should be consulted if you come across an ending which you cannot confidently identify. Part Two ("Syntax") describes the chief ways in which the various word-endings are used, and should be consulted if you are unsure how a word fits into a particular sentence. Parts Three and Four cover a mixture of other points, and are mostly useful for review rather than reference (but Section **31**, "How to Use a Latin–English Dictionary," and Section **35**, "Summary of Subjunctive Uses," may sometimes also be useful for reference).

     If you know the *name* for the Latin word or phrase which is giving trouble (e.g. if you know that it is an adjective but are not sure about its case, or if you know that it is a conditional clause or indirect statement but are uncertain about its translation), the quickest way to find the information you need is by using the index on pages 140–7.

2   *Review*, i.e. for practicing a particular point (e.g. the formation of participles, the various uses of the ablative case, the different sorts of subordinate clause, the details of indirect speech, or the ways in which the Romans expressed ideas of time and place). After studying the relevant section or paragraph, you should work through any exercise or "further examples" included in the section; these will often make it clear to you whether you have understood the point.

The numbers of *sections* are printed in bold type; the numbers of *paragraphs* are printed in ordinary type. All cross-references from one section to another give the numbers of the section and the relevant paragraph(s); for example "**11**.7" refers to **Section 11**, paragraph 7, and "**20**.1–4" refers to **Section 20**, paragraphs 1–4.

TEACHER'S INTRODUCTION

This Student's Latin Grammar is designed for reference and review, as described above in the Student's Introduction. You may want not only to encourage students to use it for documenting or refreshing their memory of the use of a particular Latin word, phrase, or clause, but also to take the whole class yourself through selected sections for oral review. Always link study of grammar, whenever possible, with work on the Latin text currently being read in class.

The book is intended for use by anyone who needs a Latin grammar of a kind midway between elementary and full, but it has been devised with two particular groups of users in mind: (1) high-school students in Latin, Levels III and IV, and college students in Intermediate Latin classes who have passed from reading facsimile Latin to reading partly or wholly unadapted texts by Roman authors, and (2) high-school students in Advanced Placement Latin classes who want to review and consolidate their fledgling knowledge of grammar before winging their way to a full reference grammar. Both groups of users will find that this Student's Grammar helps with some of the difficulties that may arise during the reading of their Latin texts and provides them with a convenient guide for reviewing systematically.

This Student's Grammar takes its basic plan, and some of its material, from the Language Information Sections of the Cambridge Latin Course but is deliberately designed to be equally accessible to users of other textbooks. Its contents have been drawn up with an eye to the grammatical requirements of the syllabuses of the College Board's Advanced Placement examinations, the ACL-NJCL National Latin Exam, and the Canadian series of advanced-level readers, called Themes in Latin Literature, which is commonly used in courses for Ontario Academic Credit and in similar courses elsewhere in North America. It probably covers, however, a wider range of linguistic features than any one syllabus. It includes all the features discussed in the Cambridge Latin Course's language notes and Language Information Sections, together with some points which occur in the Course's reading material without being explicitly discussed (e.g. causal and concessive clauses) and one or two further points that do not appear in the Course at all (e.g. **quō** with the subjunctive). If you have taken your students through the Course but been forced by lack of time to foreshorten their coverage of grammatical points, you will find (provided the omissions have not been too extensive) that this grammar offers you and them a chance to fill in some of the gaps. If you wish to add points that have not been included (e.g. **quīn**), have students copy your comments onto the blank pages which have been provided at the end of the book for additional notes.

Some linguistic points are deliberately covered from more than one point of view; for example "**nōlī**" with the infinitive appears in its appropriate place in Section **12** ("Commands"), but reappears briefly in Section **21**, which gathers together the various uses of the infinitive in summary form for study and comparison. Some material which strictly belongs more to a vocabulary list than to a grammar (e.g. lists of common prepositions, verbs governing the dative, compound verbs, etc.) has been included for the student's convenience. Sections towards the end give guidance on, and practice in, the use of a Latin–English dictionary, basic metrics, and figures of speech. Small type (sometimes accompanied by a vertical bar in the margin) has been used not only for cross-references and footnotes but also as a rough indication of points that may be regarded as more peripheral, or more advanced, than the rest; but exercise your own judgment over whether, and how far, to explore a given point with students. As the grammar is not designed for use by advanced learners, its treatment of the language is necessarily selective and at times simplified; but it is hoped that it will not be found to be seriously misleading.

Most of the linguistic features covered in this grammar (especially from Part Two onwards) are illustrated by a number of translated examples; some students find that they grasp a point more quickly and securely by studying examples than by reading a description. Also included are several exercises (mainly in Part One, e.g. Sections **1, 2, 5,** and **7**) and a large number of untranslated "further examples" (especially in Parts Two, Three, and Four) designed to give students practice in the various points covered. The vocabulary used in the examples is mainly but not wholly restricted to words which occur in the Checklists (basic-vocabulary lists) of the Cambridge Latin Course.

The book is primarily designed for students whose aim is to read and understand a Latin text or translate it into English when required. This does not mean that such points as 3rd-declension genitive plurals and the rule of "sequence of tenses," which assume extra importance for the student whose aim is to translate *into* Latin, have been omitted; but teachers whose special concern is with English-into-Latin composition may find it necessary to amplify the book's explanation of these points with further comment of their own (for which, again, the blank pages at the end may be useful).

PART ONE

MORPHOLOGY
(formation of words)

1 Nouns

1 *first declension*
puella, f.* *girl*

	SINGULAR	PLURAL
nominative and vocative	puella	puellae
genitive	puellae	puellārum
dative	puellae	puellīs
accusative	puellam	puellās
ablative	puellā	puellīs

2 *second declension*
servus, m.* *slave;* **puer,** m. *boy;* **magister,** m. *teacher;* **deus,** m. *god;* **templum,** n.* *temple:*

SINGULAR				
nominative and vocative	servus (*voc.* serve)	puer	magister	templum
genitive	servī	puerī	magistrī	templī
dative	servō	puerō	magistrō	templō
accusative	servum	puerum	magistrum	templum
ablative	servō	puerō	magistrō	templō
PLURAL				
nominative and vocative	servī	puerī	magistrī	templa
genitive	servōrum	puerōrum	magistrōrum	templōrum
dative	servīs	puerīs	magistrīs	templīs
accusative	servōs	puerōs	magistrōs	templa
ablative	servīs	puerīs	magistrīs	templīs

Some 2nd-declension nouns whose nominative and vocative singular end in **-er**, e.g. **gener**, form their endings in the same way as **puer**; others, e.g. **ager**, form their endings like **magister**.

2nd-declension nouns whose nominative singular ends in **-ius** (e.g. **fīlius**) have a vocative singular ending in **-ī** (e.g. **fīlī**).

2nd-declension nouns whose nominative ends in **-ius** or **-ium** (e.g. **fīlius, cōnsilium**) sometimes shorten the ending of their genitive singular from **-iī** to **-ī** (e.g. **fīlī** instead of **fīliī**, and **cōnsilī** instead of **cōnsiliī**).

* f. = feminine; m. = masculine; n. = neuter.

deus, m. *god* and **vir**, m. *man* have the following forms:

	SINGULAR	PLURAL	SINGULAR	PLURAL
nominative and vocative	deus	deī/dī	vir	virī
genitive	deī	deōrum/deum	virī	virōrum/virum
dative	deō	deīs/dīs	virō	virīs
accusative	deum	deos	virum	virōs
ablative	deō	deīs/dīs	virō	virīs

3 *third declension*
   mercātor, m. *merchant*; **leō**, m. *lion*; **cīvis**, m.f. *citizen*; **rēx**, m. *king*;
   urbs, f. *city*; **nōmen**, n. *name*; **tempus**, n. *time*; **mare**, n. *sea*:

SINGULAR

nom. and voc.	mercātor	leō	cīvis	rēx	urbs	nōmen	tempus	mare
gen.	mercātōris	leōnis	cīvis	rēgis	urbis	nōminis	temporis	maris
dat.	mercātōrī	leōnī	cīvī	rēgī	urbī	nōminī	temporī	marī
acc.	mercātōrem	leōnem	cīvem	rēgem	urbem	nōmen	tempus	mare
abl.	mercātōre	leōne	cīve	rēge	urbe	nōmine	tempore	marī

PLURAL

nom. and voc.	mercātōrēs	leōnēs	cīvēs	rēgēs	urbēs	nōmina	tempora	maria
gen.	mercātōrum	leōnum	cīvium	rēgum	urbium	nōminum	temporum	marium
dat.	mercātōribus	leōnibus	cīvibus	rēgibus	urbibus	nōminibus	temporibus	maribus
acc.	mercātōrēs	leōnēs	cīvēs	rēgēs	urbēs	nōmina	tempora	maria
abl.	mercātōribus	leōnibus	cīvibus	rēgibus	urbibus	nōminibus	temporibus	maribus

3rd-declension nouns form their genitive plural in the following ways:
  (i) nouns whose genitive singular contains more syllables than their
      nominative singular (e.g. **leō**, genitive **leōnis**) have a genitive plural
      ending in **-um** (e.g. **leōnum**).
      Exceptions: nouns whose nominative singular contains only one
      syllable and which have two consonants before the **-is** of their
      genitive singular (e.g. **mōns**, genitive **montis**) have a genitive plural
      ending in **-ium** (e.g. **montium**).
  (ii) nouns whose genitive singular has the same number of syllables as
      their nominative singular (e.g. **cīvis**, genitive **cīvis**) have a genitive
      plural ending in **-ium** (e.g. **cīvium**).
      Exceptions: **pater, māter, frāter, senex, iuvenis** and **canis** have a
      genitive plural ending in **-um** (e.g. **patrum**).

3rd-declension neuter nouns whose nominative singular ends in **-e, -al** or
-ar (e.g. **conclāve, animal**) change their endings in the same way as
mare. Their ablative singular ends in **-ī** (e.g. **conclāvī, animālī**) and their ·
genitive plural ends in **-ium** (e.g. **conclāvium, animālium**).

4 *fourth declension*
manus, f. *hand* and **genū**, n. *knee*

	SINGULAR	PLURAL	SINGULAR	PLURAL
nominative and vocative	manus	manūs	genū	genua
genitive	manūs	manuum	genūs	genuum
dative	manuī	manibus	genū	genibus
accusative	manum	manūs	genū	genua
ablative	manū	manibus	genū	genibus

The irregular noun **domus**, f. *house, home* has the following forms:

	SINGULAR	PLURAL
nominative and vocative	domus	domūs
genitive	domūs	domuum/domōrum
dative	domuī	domibus
accusative	domum	domūs/domōs
ablative	domō	domibus

5 *fifth declension*
diēs, m. *day* and **rēs**, f. *thing, business, affair*

	SINGULAR	PLURAL	SINGULAR	PLURAL
nominative and vocative	diēs	diēs	rēs	rēs
genitive	diēī	diērum	reī	rērum
dative	diēī	diēbus	reī	rēbus
accusative	diem	diēs	rem	rēs
ablative	diē	diēbus	rē	rēbus

6 For examples of ways in which the different cases are used, see **14**.1–6.

7 With the help of paragraphs 1–5, and of **14**.1–6, work out the Latin for the italicized words:

1 We soon entered the *city*.
2 The governor provided a ship for the *merchants*.
3 The mother of the *girl* lived nearby.
4 The visitor was admiring the *temples*.
5 Come here, *slave*!
6 The *lions* were lying under a tree.
7 It was now the third hour of the *day*.
8 I handed the *boy* a wax tablet.
9 An attendant read out the *citizens'* names.
10 This letter was written by the *hand* of the *king* himself.

8   Sometimes the plural of a noun is used with a singular meaning, especially in verse:

> **per amīca** *silentia* **lūnae**
> *through the friendly* **silence** *of the moonlight*

9   The gender of a Latin noun depends

    (i) partly on its meaning:
       nouns referring to males   – masculine
       nouns referring to females   – feminine
       nouns referring to things   – masculine, feminine or neuter

   (ii) partly on its declension:
       most 1st- and 5th-declension nouns   – feminine
       most 2nd- and 4th-declension nouns ending in **-us** – masculine
       all 2nd-declension nouns ending in **-um**
       and 4th-declension nouns ending in **-ū**   – neuter

  (iii) partly on the ending of the nominative singular. For example:
       most 3rd-declension nouns ending in **-or**   – masculine
       many 3rd-declension nouns ending in **-is**   – feminine
       However, the ending of the nominative singular is only a rough guide to the gender of a noun, and cannot be relied on as a fixed rule. When in doubt, look up the nominative form in a Latin dictionary, where the gender will be identified.

10   Some place-names have a *locative* case, formed in the following ways:

	nominative	locative
1st-declension: singular	**Rōma** *Rome*	**Rōmae** *at Rome*
plural	**Athēnae** *Athens*	**Athēnīs** *at Athens*
2nd-declension: singular	**Londinium** *London*	**Londiniī** *in London*
plural	**Philippī** *Philippi*	**Philippīs** *at Philippi*
3rd-declension: singular	**Neapolis** *Naples*	**Neapolī/Neapole** *at Naples*
plural	**Gādēs** *Cadiz*	**Gādibus** *at Cadiz*

The nouns **domus, humus,** and **rūs** have locatives **domī** *at home,* **humī** *on the ground,* and **rūrī** *in the countryside.*

For examples of the way the locative case is used, see **15.2d(iii).**

2   Adjectives

1   *first and second declension*
bonus *good;* **pulcher** *beautiful;* **miser** *unhappy:*

	masculine	*feminine*	*neuter*	*masculine*	*feminine*	*neuter*
SINGULAR						
nominative and vocative	bonus (*voc.* bone)	bona	bonum	pulcher	pulchra	pulchrum
genitive	bonī	bonae	bonī	pulchrī	pulchrae	pulchrī
dative	bonō	bonae	bonō	pulchrō	pulchrae	pulchrō
accusative	bonum	bonam	bonum	pulchrum	pulchram	pulchrum
ablative	bonō	bonā	bonō	pulchrō	pulchrā	pulchrō
PLURAL						
nominative and vocative	bonī	bonae	bona	pulchrī	pulchrae	pulchra
genitive	bonōrum	bonārum	bonōrum	pulchrōrum	pulchrārum	pulchrōrum
dative	bonīs	bonīs	bonīs	pulchrīs	pulchrīs	pulchrīs
accusative	bonōs	bonās	bona	pulchrōs	pulchrās	pulchra
ablative	bonīs	bonīs	bonīs	pulchrīs	pulchrīs	pulchrīs

	masculine	*feminine*	*neuter*
SINGULAR			
nominative and vocative	miser	misera	miserum
genitive	miserī	miserae	miserī
dative	miserō	miserae	miserō
accusative	miserum	miseram	miserum
ablative	miserō	miserā	miserō
PLURAL			
nominative and vocative	miserī	miserae	misera
genitive	miserōrum	miserārum	miserōrum
dative	miserīs	miserīs	miserīs
accusative	miserōs	miserās	misera
ablative	miserīs	miserīs	miserīs

13

2 *third declension*
ācer *eager; excited;* **fortis** *brave;* **fēlīx** *lucky;* **ingēns** *huge;* **vetus** *old:*

	masculine	feminine	neuter	masc. and fem.	neuter	masc. and fem.	neuter
SINGULAR							
nominative and vocative	ācer	ācris	ācre	fortis	forte	fēlīx	fēlīx
genitive	ācris	ācris	ācris	fortis	fortis	fēlīcis	fēlīcis
dative	ācrī	ācrī	ācrī	fortī	fortī	fēlīcī	fēlīcī
accusative	ācrem	ācrem	ācre	fortem	forte	fēlīcem	fēlīx
ablative	ācrī	ācrī	ācrī	fortī	fortī	fēlīcī	fēlīcī
PLURAL							
nominative and vocative	ācrēs	ācrēs	ācria	fortēs	fortia	fēlīcēs	fēlīcia
genitive	ācrium	ācrium	ācrium	fortium	fortium	fēlīcium	fēlīcium
dative	ācribus	ācribus	ācribus	fortibus	fortibus	fēlīcibus	fēlīcibus
accusative	ācrēs	ācrēs	ācria	fortēs	fortia	fēlīcēs	fēlīcia
ablative	ācribus	ācribus	ācribus	fortibus	fortibus	fēlīcibus	fēlīcibus

	masc. and fem.	neuter	masc. and fem.	neuter
SINGULAR				
nominative and vocative	ingēns	ingēns	vetus	vetus
genitive	ingentis	ingentis	veteris	veteris
dative	ingentī	ingentī	veterī	veterī
accusative	ingentem	ingēns	veterem	vetus
ablative	ingent **-ī/-e**	ingent **-ī/-e**	vetere	vetere
PLURAL				
nominative and vocative	ingentēs	ingentia	veterēs	vetera
genitive	ingentium	ingentium	veterum	veterum
dative	ingentibus	ingentibus	veteribus	veteribus
accusative	ingentēs	ingentia	veterēs	vetera
ablative	ingentibus	ingentibus	veteribus	veteribus

A few adjectives of participial origin (e.g. **prūdēns**) or participles used as adjectives (cf. **7f.3**) usually have an **-ī** ending in the ablative singular when they modify a stated noun, e.g. **ā servō ingentī** *by the huge slave;* they generally have an **-e** ending in the ablative singular when they describe a noun not stated, but understood, e.g. **ab ingente** *by the huge (person).*

A few adjectives (e.g. **dīves, pauper**) change their endings in the same way as **vetus**. Their ablative singular ends in **-e** (e.g. **dīvite, paupere**) and their genitive plural ends in **-um** (e.g. **dīvitum, pauperum**).

For an example of the way in which *comparative* adjectives change their endings, see **lātior** in **4.1**.

3 For examples of agreement between adjectives and nouns, see **17**.2.

4 For examples of adjectives used attributively and predicatively, see **18**.1–7.

5 For examples of various types of word order involving nouns and adjectives, see **29**.1–7.

6 *Exercise* With the help of **1**.1–5, paragraphs 1 and 2 above and **14**.1–6, work out the Latin for the italicized words:

1 I gave a reward to the *brave citizen*.
2 The visitors admired the *beautiful temples*.
3 The *unhappy merchants* returned home.
4 We listened to the words of the *fortunate boy*.
5 They were startled by a *huge shout*.
   (*clāmor* changes its endings in the same way as *mercātor*.)
6 The deeds of *good kings* are never forgotten.

7 Masculine, feminine and neuter forms of adjectives can be used on their own (i.e. unaccompanied by nouns) with the meanings ". . . man, men," ". . . woman, women," and ". . . thing, things":

bonus	*a good man*	**nostrī**	*our men*
multae	*many women*	**vēra**	*true things*
omnia	*all things, everything*		(i.e. *the truth*)

3 Adverbs

Formed from adjectives in the following ways:

adjective	*adverb*
first and second declension	
lātus *wide* (genitive **lātī**)	**lātē** *widely*
pulcher *beautiful* (gen. **pulchrī**)	**pulchrē** *beautifully*
third declension	
fortis *brave* (gen. **fortis**)	**fortiter** *bravely*
fēlīx *lucky* (gen. **fēlīcis**)	**fēlīciter** *luckily*
prūdēns *shrewd* (gen. **prūdentis**)	**prūdenter** *shrewdly*

A few third-declension adjectives, such as **facilis** *easy*, form adverbs ending in **-e**, e.g. **facile** *easily*.

4 Comparison

1 comparison of adjectives

positive (i.e. the "normal" form of the adjective)	comparative	superlative
lātus	**lātior**	**lātissimus**
wide	*wider*	*widest, very wide*
pulcher	**pulchrior**	**pulcherrimus**
beautiful	*more beautiful*	*most beautiful, very beautiful*
fortis	**fortior**	**fortissimus**
brave	*braver*	*bravest, very brave*
fēlīx	**fēlīcior**	**fēlīcissimus**
lucky	*luckier*	*luckiest, very lucky*
prūdēns	**prūdentior**	**prūdentissimus**
shrewd	*shrewder*	*shrewdest, very shrewd*
facilis	**facilior**	**facillimus***
easy	*easier*	*easiest, very easy*

Irregular forms:

bonus	**melior**	**optimus**
good	*better*	*best, very good*
malus	**peior**	**pessimus**
bad	*worse*	*worst, very bad*
magnus	**maior**	**maximus**
big	*bigger*	*biggest, very big*
parvus	**minor**	**minimus**
small	*smaller*	*smallest, very small*
multus	**plūs**	**plūrimus**
much	*more*	*most, very much*
multī	**plūrēs**	**plūrimī**
many	*more*	*most, very many*

Comparative adjectives such as **lātior** change their endings in the following way:

	SINGULAR		PLURAL	
	masc. and fem.	*neuter*	*masc. and fem.*	*neuter*
nominative and vocative	**lātior**	**lātius**	**lātiōrēs**	**lātiōra**
genitive	**lātiōris**	**lātiōris**	**lātiōrum**	**lātiōrum**
dative	**lātiōrī**	**lātiōrī**	**lātiōribus**	**lātiōribus**
accusative	**lātiōrem**	**lātius**	**lātiōrēs**	**lātiōra**
ablative	**lātiōre**	**lātiōre**	**lātiōribus**	**lātiōribus**

Superlative adjectives such as **lātissimus** change their endings in the same way as **bonus** (shown in **2.1**).

> **plūs**, the comparative form of **multus** listed above, is a neuter singular noun meaning "more, a greater quantity" and is often used with the genitive, e.g. **plūs cibī** "more (of) food."

* The adjectives **difficilis, similis, dissimilis, gracilis**, and **humilis** form their superlative in the same way as **facilis**, e.g. **difficillimus, simillimus**, etc.

2 Comparison of adverbs

positive	comparative	superlative
lātē	**lātius**	**lātissimē**
widely	*more widely*	*most widely, very widely*
pulchrē	**pulchrius**	**pulcherrimē**
beautifully	*more beautifully*	*most beautifully, very beautifully*
fortiter	**fortius**	**fortissimē**
bravely	*more bravely*	*most bravely, very bravely*
fēlīciter	**fēlīcius**	**fēlīcissimē**
luckily	*more luckily*	*most luckily, very luckily*
prūdenter	**prūdentius**	**prūdentissimē**
shrewdly	*more shrewdly*	*most shrewdly, very shrewdly*
facile	**facilius**	**facillimē**
easily	*more easily*	*most easily, very easily*

Irregular forms:

bene	**melius**	**optimē**
well	*better*	*best, very well*
male	**peius**	**pessimē**
badly	*worse*	*worst, very badly*
magnopere	**magis**	**maximē**
greatly	*more*	*most, very greatly*
paulum	**minus**	**minimē**
little	*less*	*least, very little*
multum	**plūs**	**plūrimum**
much	*more*	*most, very much*

3 Comparative forms are sometimes used with the meaning "too . . ." or "rather . . .":

in mediā palaestrā stābat āthlēta *altior*.
*In the middle of the exercise area stood a **rather tall** athlete*
(i.e. *an athlete **taller** than average*).

mercātor iter *lentius* faciēbat.
*The merchant was traveling **too slowly** (i.e. **more slowly** than he should*
have done).

4 Superlative forms are sometimes used with **quam**, meaning "as . . . as possible":

quam celerrimē	*as quickly as possible*
quam maximus	*as large as possible*

5 Pronouns*

1 ego, tū, nōs, and vōs (*I, you* (sg.), *we, you* (pl.))

	SINGULAR		PLURAL	
nominative	ego	tū	nōs	vōs
genitive	meī	tuī	nostrum/nostrī	vestrum/vestrī
dative	mihi	tibi	nōbīs	vōbīs
accusative	mē	tē	nōs	vōs
ablative	mē	tē	nōbīs	vōbīs

sē (*herself, himself, itself, themselves,* etc.)

	SINGULAR	PLURAL
	masc., fem., and neuter	*masc., fem., and neuter*
nominative (no forms)		
genitive	suī	suī
dative	sibi	sibi
accusative	sē	sē
ablative	sē	sē

mīlitēs *sē* **īnstrūxērunt.**	*The soldiers drew **themselves** up.*
senex cēnam *sibi* **coxit.**	*The old man cooked a dinner **for himself**.*
	*Or, The old man cooked **himself** a dinner.*

(Compare these examples with the way **ipse** (paragraph 5) is used.)

Further examples:

1 fūr sub mēnsā sē cēlāvit.
2 captīvī sē interfēcērunt.
3 puella sibi equum ēmit.

For examples of **sē** used in indirect statements, see **25.4d**.**

When **cum** *with* is used with one of the above pronouns, it is written after the pronoun, in one word. For example:

mēcum	*with me*
vōbīscum	*with you* (plural)
sēcum	*with him(self)*
	with them(selves)

---

* **nostrum** and **vestrum**, express a whole of which someone or something is a part, e.g. **unus vestrum** *one of you;* **nostrī** and **vestrī** have the same relation to a noun or adjective as that of an object to a verb, e.g. **timor nostrī** *fear of us (felt towards us).*

** including some pronominal adjectives (i.e. adjectives related to pronouns).

The possessive adjectives related to these pronouns are:

meus[†]   *my*
tuus   *your* (referring to one person)
noster   *our*
vester   *your* (referring to more than one person)
suus   *his (own), her (own), its (own), their (own)*

vīlla mea ardēbat.	*My house was on fire.*
amīcōs vestrōs vīdistis?	*Have you (pl.) seen your friends?*
patrem suum necāvit.	*He killed his (own) father.*
cibum līberīs suīs dedērunt.	*They gave food to their (own) children.*

(Compare the last two examples with the two examples at the end of paragraph 6 below.)

2   **hic** (*this, these,* etc.; also used with the meanings "he," "she," "it," "they," etc.)

	SINGULAR			PLURAL		
	masculine	*feminine*	*neuter*	*masculine*	*feminine*	*neuter*
nominative	**hic**	**haec**	**hoc**	**hī**	**hae**	**haec**
genitive	**huius**	**huius**	**huius**	**hōrum**	**hārum**	**hōrum**
dative	**huic**	**huic**	**huic**	**hīs**	**hīs**	**hīs**
accusative	**hunc**	**hanc**	**hoc**	**hōs**	**hās**	**haec**
ablative	**hōc**	**hāc**	**hōc**	**hīs**	**hīs**	**hīs**

3   **ille** *that, those,* etc.; also used with the meaning "he," "she," "it," "they," etc.)

	SINGULAR			PLURAL		
	masculine	*feminine*	*neuter*	*masculine*	*feminine*	*neuter*
nominative	**ille**	**illa**	**illud**	**illī**	**illae**	**illa**
genitive	**illīus**	**illīus**	**illīus**	**illōrum**	**illārum**	**illōrum**
dative	**illī**	**illī**	**illī**	**illīs**	**illīs**	**illīs**
accusative	**illum**	**illam**	**illud**	**illōs**	**illās**	**illa**
ablative	**illō**	**illā**	**illō**	**illīs**	**illīs**	**illīs**

[†] vocative masculine singular **mī**.

4 **iste** (*that, that . . . of yours,* etc.; sometimes used in an uncomplimentary way) changes its endings in the same way as **ille**:

	SINGULAR			PLURAL		
	masculine	*feminine*	*neuter*	*masculine*	*feminine*	*neuter*
nominative	iste	ista	istud	istī	istae	ista
genitive	istīus	istīus	istīus	istōrum	istārum	istōrum
dative	istī	istī	istī	istīs	istīs	istīs
accusative	istum	istam	istud	istōs	istās	ista
ablative	istō	istā	istō	istīs	istīs	istīs

istud aedificium   *that building of yours*
iste canis   *that wretched dog*

5 **ipse** (*myself, yourself, himself, itself, themselves,* etc.)

	SINGULAR			PLURAL		
	masculine	*feminine*	*neuter*	*masculine*	*feminine*	*neuter*
nominative	ipse	ipsa	ipsum	ipsī	ipsae	ipsa
genitive	ipsīus	ipsīus	ipsīus	ipsōrum	ipsārum	ipsōrum
dative	ipsī	ipsī	ipsī	ipsīs	ipsīs	ipsīs
accusative	ipsum	ipsam	ipsum	ipsōs	ipsās	ipsa
ablative	ipsō	ipsā	ipsō	ipsīs	ipsīs	ipsīs

rēx *ipse* lacrimābat.   *The king **himself** was weeping.*
fēmina mē *ipsum* accūsāvit.   *The woman accused me **myself**.*
cōnsulēs *ipsī* aderant.   *The consuls **themselves** were there.*

(Compare these examples with the way **sē** (paragraph 1) is used.)

Further examples:

1 ego ipse centuriōnem servāvī.
2 vōs ipsī in tabernā bibēbātis.
3 subitō gladiātōrēs ipsōs vīdimus.
4 dea ipsa mihi appāruit.
5 haec est statua ipsīus Caesaris.

6 **is** (*he, she, it,* etc.; also used with the meaning "that," "those," etc.)

	SINGULAR			PLURAL		
	masculine	*feminine*	*neuter*	*masculine*	*feminine*	*neuter*
nominative	is	ea	id	eī/iī	eae	ea
genitive	eius	eius	eius	eōrum	eārum	eōrum
dative	eī	eī	eī	eīs/iīs	eīs/iīs	eīs/iīs
accusative	eum	eam	id	eōs	eās	ea
ablative	eō	eā	eō	eīs/iīs	eīs/iīs	eīs/iīs

For examples in which forms of **is** are used with the relative pronoun **quī**, see **23**.1.

The genitive singular and plural forms of **is** can be used to mean "his," "her," "its," and "their":

patrem *eius* necāvit.
*He killed **his** (i.e. someone else's) father.*

cibum līberīs *eōrum* dedērunt.
*They gave food to **their** (i.e. other people's) children.*

(Compare these examples with the last two examples in paragraph above.)

7   **īdem** *the same*

	SINGULAR			PLURAL		
	masculine	*feminine*	*neuter*	*masculine*	*feminine*	*neuter*
nominative	**īdem**	**eadem**	**idem**	**eīdem/īdem**	**eaedem**	**eadem**
genitive	**eiusdem**	**eiusdem**	**eiusdem**	**eōrundem**	**eārundem**	**eōrundem**
dative	**eīdem**	**eīdem**	**eīdem**	**eīsdem/īsdem**	**eīsdem/īsdem**	**eīsdem/īsdem**
accusative	**eundem**	**eandem**	**idem**	**eōsdem**	**eāsdem**	**eadem**
ablative	**eōdem**	**eādem**	**eōdem**	**eīsdem/īsdem**	**eīsdem/īsdem**	**eīsdem/īsdem**

eōsdem puerōs postrīdiē audīvērunt.
*They heard **the same** boys on the next day.*

haec est *eiusdem* fēminae domus.
*This is the house **of the same** woman.*

Further examples:

1 eandem puellam iterum vīdimus.
2 nūntius eōdem diē revēnit.
3 eīdem servī in agrīs labōrābant.

8   The relative pronoun **quī** (*who, which,* etc.)

	SINGULAR			PLURAL		
	masculine	*feminine*	*neuter*	*masculine*	*feminine*	*neuter*
nominative	**quī**	**quae**	**quod**	**quī**	**quae**	**quae**
genitive	**cuius**	**cuius**	**cuius**	**quōrum**	**quārum**	**quōrum**
dative	**cui**	**cui**	**cui**	**quibus/quīs**	**quibus/quīs**	**quibus/quīs**
accusative	**quem**	**quam**	**quod**	**quōs**	**quās**	**quae**
ablative	**quō**	**quā**	**quō**	**quibus/quīs**	**quibus/quīs**	**quibus/quīs**

For examples of agreement between the relative pronoun and a noun or pronoun, see **17**.4.
For examples of clauses introduced by forms of **quī**, see **23**.1.

Forms of **quī** can also be used at the start of sentences, with the meaning "he," "this," etc. (this is known as the *connecting* use of the relative pronoun):

> **tertiā hōrā dux advēnit.** *quem* **cum cōnspexissent, mīlitēs magnum clāmōrem sustulērunt.**
> *At the third hour the leader arrived. When they caught sight of **him**, the soldiers raised a great shout.*

> **deinde nūntiī locūtī sunt.** *quōrum* **verbīs obstupefactus, rēx diū tacēbat.**
> *Then the messengers spoke. Stunned by **their** words, the king was silent for a long time.*

> **pontifex ipse templum dēdicāvit.** *quō* **factō, omnēs plausērunt.**
> *The chief priest himself dedicated the temple. When **this** had been done, everybody applauded.*

Further examples:

1 rēx mihi signum dedit. quod simulac vīdī, victimam ad āram dūxī.
2 iūdex "hic vir," inquit, "est innocēns." quibus verbīs audītīs, spectātōrēs īrātissimī erant.
3 dominus ancillam ad forum mīsit. quae, cum cibum comparāvisset, ad vīllam celeriter revēnit.

> The syllable **quī**, in **aliquī** *some*, **quīcumque** *whoever, whichever*, etc. and **quī . . . ?** *which . . . ?* changes its endings in the same way as the relative pronoun:
>
> | | |
> |---|---|
> | *quī* **puer fēcit?** | *Which boy did this?* |
> | *aliquod* **crīmen** | *some accusation* |
> | *quaecumque* **prōvincia** | *whatever province* |

9 quīdam (*one, a certain*)

	SINGULAR			PLURAL		
	masculine	*feminine*	*neuter*	*masculine*	*feminine*	*neuter*
nominative	quīdam	quaedam	quoddam	quīdam	quaedam	quaedam
genitive	cuiusdam	cuiusdam	cuiusdam	quōrundam	quārundam	quōrundam
dative	cuidam	cuidam	cuidam	quibusdam	quibusdam	quibusdam
accusative	quendam	quandam	quoddam	quōsdam	quāsdam	quaedam
ablative	quōdam	quādam	quōdam	quibusdam	quibusdam	quibusdam

> **mīlitem** *quendam* **dormientem animadvertit.**
> *He noticed **one** soldier sleeping.*

> **in vīllā** *cuiusdam* **amīcī manēbāmus.**
> *We were staying in the villa **of a certain** friend.*

Further examples:

1 fēminae quaedam extrā iānuam stābant.
2 senātor quīdam subitō surrēxit.
3 quōsdam hominēs in forō cōnspexī.

10 **quis? quid?** (*who? what?*)

| | SINGULAR | | | PLURAL | | |
	masculine	feminine	neuter	masculine	feminine	neuter
nominative	**quis**	**quis**	**quid**	**quī**	**quae**	**quae**
genitive	**cuius**	**cuius**	**cuius**	**quōrum**	**quārum**	**quōrum**
dative	**cui**	**cui**	**cui**	**quibus**	**quibus**	**quibus**
accusative	**quem**	**quam**	**quid**	**quōs**	**quās**	**quae**
ablative	**quō**	**quā**	**quō**	**quibus**	**quibus**	**quibus**

The forms of **quis** can also be used with **sī**, **nisi**, **nē**, and **num** to mean "anyone," "anything":

sī *quis* restiterit, comprehende eum!
*If **anybody** resists, arrest him!*

centuriō mē rogāvit num *quid* vīdissem.
*The centurion asked me whether I had seen **anything**.*

> *The syllable* **quis**, *in* **quisque** *each*, **quisquam** *any*, used after negative words, **quisquis** *whoever* and **aliquis**, **aliquid** *someone, something*, changes its endings in the same way as **quis?**:
>
> | | |
> |---|---|
> | ***quidquid* accidit, semper rīdet.** | *Whatever happens, he always smiles.* |
> | ***aliquis* clāmābat.** | *Someone was shouting.* |
> | **neque *quemquam* vīdī.** | *Nor did I see **anybody**.* |
> | | Or, in more natural English: |
> | | *And I didn't see **anybody**.* |
> | **prō sē *quisque* pugnābat.** | *Each one was fighting for himself.* |
>
> **quisque** is also used with superlative adjectives in the following way:
>
> | | |
> |---|---|
> | **optimus *quisque*** | *each very good man*, i.e. *all the best men* |
> | **celerrimus *quisque*** | *each very fast person*, i.e. *all the fastest people* |

11 The following words change most of their endings in the same way as 1st and 2nd declension adjectives like **bonus, pulcher,** and **miser** (shown in **2.**1), but have a genitive singular ending in **-īus** and a dative singular ending in **-ī**:

ūnus	*one* (shown in full in **6.**1)		
nūllus	*no, none*	**alter**	*the other* (of two)
sōlus	*alone*	**alius***	*another*
tōtus	*whole*	**uter?**	*which* (of two)?
ūllus	*any*	**neuter**	*neither*

uterque *each, both* has genitive singular **utrīusque** and dative singular **utrīque**.

12 **nēmō** (*no one*)

nominative	**nēmō**
genitive	**nūllīus**
dative	**nēminī**
accusative	**nēminem**
ablative	**nūllō**

13 *Exercise*   With the help of paragraphs 1–12, work out the Latin for the italicized words:

1 *That* old man is the consul.
2 *What* has happened?
3 I found *no one* there.
4 We were detained in the city by *certain* business (*negōtium* is neuter).
5 The queen stabbed *herself.*
6 The soldiers seized the queen *herself.*
7 I again gave my message, to *the same* slave as before.
8 He ran after the men, but couldn't catch *them.*
9 Where is *this* horse's owner?
10 I will tell *you* the reason, my friends.
11 Three slave-girls ran up, with *whose* help the fire was extinguished.
12 He became king of the *whole* island.
13 I was bitten by *that* dog *of yours.*
14 *One* merchant was doing very good business.

---

*nominative, vocative, and accusative neuter singular **aliud**

6   Numerals

1	I	ūnus	1	XX	vīgintī	20
	II	duo	2	XXX	trīgintā	30
	III	trēs	3	XL	quadrāgintā	40
	IV	quattuor	4	L	quīnquāgintā	50
	V	quīnque	5	LX	sexāgintā	60
	VI	sex	6	LXX	septuāgintā	70
	VII	septem	7	LXXX	octōgintā	80
	VIII	octō	8	XC	nōnāgintā	90
	IX	novem	9	C	centum	100
	X	decem	10	CC	ducentī	200
	XI	ūndecim	11	CCC	trecentī	300
	XII	duodecim	12	CCCC	quadringentī	400
	XIII	trēdecim	13	D	quīngentī	500
	XIV	quattuordecim	14	DC	sescentī	600
	XV	quīndecim	15	DCC	septingentī	700
	XVI	sēdecim	16	DCCC	octingentī	800
	XVII	septendecim	17	DCCCC	nōngentī	900
	XVIII	duodēvīgintī	18	M	mīlle	1000
	XIX	ūndēvīgintī	19	MM	duo mīlia	2000

Compound numbers below 100 (e.g. 46, 63, 95) can be formed *either* with the smaller number first, followed by **et** and the larger number, *or* with the larger number first, followed by the smaller number without **et**:

quīnque et trīgintā or **trīgintā quīnque**   35
septem et octōgintā or **octōgintā septem**   87*

28, 29, 38, 39, 48, 49, etc. are usually formed as follows:

duodētrīgintā   28   **ūndētrīgintā**   29
duodēquadrāgintā 38   **ūndēquadrāgintā**   39   etc.†

In compound numbers above 100, the larger number is placed in front of the smaller number, with or without **et**:

ducentī et sex or **ducentī sex**   206

ūnus, duo, and **trēs** change their endings in the following way:

	masculine	*feminine*	*neuter*	*masculine*	*feminine*	*neuter*
nominative	ūnus	ūna	ūnum	duo	duae	duo
genitive	ūnīus	ūnīus	ūnīus	duōrum	duārum	duōrum
dative	ūnī	ūnī	ūnī	duōbus	duābus	duōbus
accusative	ūnum	ūnam	ūnum	duōs/duo	duās	duo
ablative	ūnō	ūnā	ūnō	duōbus	duābus	duōbus

ambō *both* changes its endings in the same way as **duo.**

* **ūnus** is generally placed first:
ūnus et quīnquāgintā   51

† But **octō et nōnāgintā**
Or **nōnāgintā octō**   98   **ūndēcentum**   99

	masc. and fem.	neuter
nominative	**trēs**	**tria**
genitive	**trium**	**trium**
dative	**tribus**	**tribus**
accusative	**trēs**	**tria**
ablative	**tribus**	**tribus**

The numbers from **quattuor** to **centum** do not change their endings. **ducentī, trecentī**, etc. change their endings in the same way as the plural of **bonus** (shown in **2.1**).

mīlle does not change its endings:

> *mīlle* **servī**   *a **thousand** slaves*
> **cum** *mīlle* **servīs**   *with a **thousand** slaves*

mīlia changes its endings in the same way as the plural of **mare** (shown in **1.3**), and is used with a noun in the genitive case:

> **sex** *mīlia* **servōrum**   *six **thousand(s)** (of) slaves*
> **cum sex** *mīlibus* **servōrum**   *with six **thousand(s)** (of) slaves*

2

prīmus	*first*	**sextus**	*sixth*
secundus	*second*	**septimus**	*seventh*
tertius	*third*	**octāvus**	*eighth*
quārtus	*fourth*	**nōnus**	*ninth*
quīntus	*fifth*	**decimus**	*tenth*

prīmus, secundus, etc. change their endings in the same way as **bonus** (shown in **2.1**).

3

singulī	*one each*	**sēnī**	*six each*
bīnī	*two each*	**septēnī**	*seven each*
ternī	*three each*	**octōnī**	*eight each*
quaternī	*four each*	**novēnī**	*nine each*
quīnī	*five each*	**dēnī**	*ten each*

These numbers change their endings in the same way as the plural of **bonus** (shown in **2.1**).

4

semel	*once*	**sexiēs**	*six times*
bis	*twice*	**septiēs**	*seven times*
ter	*three times*	**octiēs**	*eight times*
quater	*four times*	**noviēs**	*nine times*
quīnquiēs	*five times*	**deciēs**	*ten times*

7 Verbs

7a Summary of verb forms

sg. = singular   pl. = plural
1, 2, 3 = 1st, 2nd, and 3rd person (meaning "I . . .," "you . . .," and "s/he,"
"it . . .," in the singular, and "we . . .," "you . . .," and "they . . ." in the
plural)

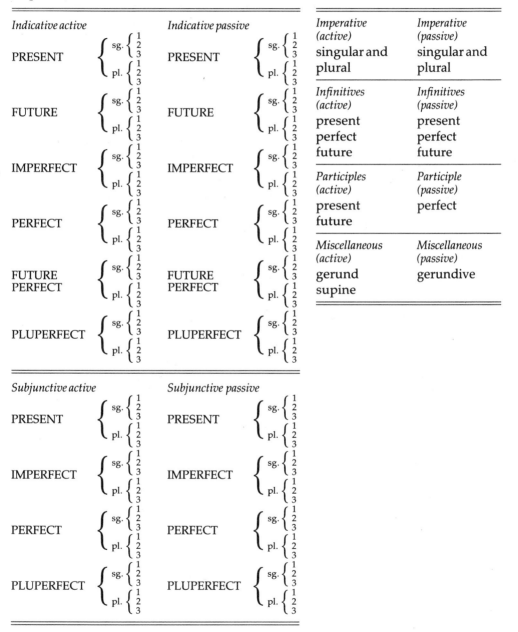

Indicative active

PRESENT — sg. 1 2 3 / pl. 1 2 3

FUTURE — sg. 1 2 3 / pl. 1 2 3

IMPERFECT — sg. 1 2 3 / pl. 1 2 3

PERFECT — sg. 1 2 3 / pl. 1 2 3

FUTURE PERFECT — sg. 1 2 3 / pl. 1 2 3

PLUPERFECT — sg. 1 2 3 / pl. 1 2 3

Indicative passive

PRESENT — sg. 1 2 3 / pl. 1 2 3

FUTURE — sg. 1 2 3 / pl. 1 2 3

IMPERFECT — sg. 1 2 3 / pl. 1 2 3

PERFECT — sg. 1 2 3 / pl. 1 2 3

FUTURE PERFECT — sg. 1 2 3 / pl. 1 2 3

PLUPERFECT — sg. 1 2 3 / pl. 1 2 3

Imperative (active)	*Imperative (passive)*
singular and plural	singular and plural

Infinitives (active)	*Infinitives (passive)*
present	present
perfect	perfect
future	future

Participles (active)	*Participle (passive)*
present	perfect
future	

Miscellaneous (active)	*Miscellaneous (passive)*
gerund	gerundive
supine	

Subjunctive active

PRESENT — sg. 1 2 3 / pl. 1 2 3

IMPERFECT — sg. 1 2 3 / pl. 1 2 3

PERFECT — sg. 1 2 3 / pl. 1 2 3

PLUPERFECT — sg. 1 2 3 / pl. 1 2 3

Subjunctive passive

PRESENT — sg. 1 2 3 / pl. 1 2 3

IMPERFECT — sg. 1 2 3 / pl. 1 2 3

PERFECT — sg. 1 2 3 / pl. 1 2 3

PLUPERFECT — sg. 1 2 3 / pl. 1 2 3

7b Indicative Active forms of:

portō	"I carry"	audiō	"I hear"		trahō	"I drag"
doceō	"I teach"	capiō	"I take, I capture"			

1*

first conjugation	second conjugation	third conjugation	third "-iō" conjugation	fourth conjugation
PRESENT *(I carry, I am carrying, etc.)*				
port**ō**	doce**ō**	trah**ō**	cap**iō**	aud**iō**
port**ās**	doc**ēs**	trah**is**	cap**is**	aud**īs**
port**at**	doc**et**	trah**it**	cap**it**	aud**it**
port**āmus**	doc**ēmus**	trah**imus**	cap**imus**	aud**īmus**
port**ātis**	doc**ētis**	trah**itis**	cap**itis**	aud**ītis**
port**ant**	doc**ent**	trah**unt**	cap**iunt**	aud**iunt**
FUTURE *(I shall/will carry, etc.)*				
port**ābō**	doc**ēbō**	trah**am**	cap**iam**	aud**iam**
port**ābis**	doc**ēbis**	trah**ēs**	cap**iēs**	aud**iēs**
port**ābit**	doc**ēbit**	trah**et**	cap**iet**	aud**iet**
port**ābimus**	doc**ēbimus**	trah**ēmus**	cap**iēmus**	aud**iēmus**
port**ābitis**	doc**ēbitis**	trah**ētis**	cap**iētis**	aud**iētis**
port**ābunt**	doc**ēbunt**	trah**ent**	cap**ient**	aud**ient**
IMPERFECT *(I was carrying, I used to carry, I began to carry, etc.)*				
port**ābam**	doc**ēbam**	trah**ēbam**	cap**iēbam**	aud**iēbam**
port**ābās**	doc**ēbās**	trah**ēbās**	cap**iēbās**	aud**iēbās**
port**ābat**	doc**ēbat**	trah**ēbat**	cap**iēbat**	aud**iēbat**
port**ābāmus**	doc**ēbāmus**	trah**ēbāmus**	cap**iēbāmus**	aud**iēbāmus**
port**ābātis**	doc**ēbātis**	trah**ēbātis**	cap**iēbātis**	aud**iēbātis**
port**ābant**	doc**ēbant**	trah**ēbant**	cap**iēbant**	aud**iēbant**

2 **capiō** belongs to a group of verbs which form some of their endings like third-conjugation verbs such as **trahō** but form other endings like fourth-conjugation verbs such as **audiō**. (Other common verbs in this group are **faciō**, **iaciō**, and **rapiō**; for further examples, see 36.4.)

3 The *historical* use of the present tense (*"historical present"* for short) is often employed by Roman writers as a lively or vivid way of describing events that happened in the past:

> **fūr per fenestram intrāvit. circumspexit; sed omnia tacita erant. subitō sonitum** *audit;* **ē tablīnō canis sē** *praecipitat.* **fūr effugere cōnātur;** *lātrat* **canis;** *irrumpunt* **servī et fūrem** *comprehendunt.*

> *A thief entered through the window. He looked around; but all was silent. Suddenly he **hears** a noise; a dog **charges** out of the study. The thief **tries** to escape; the dog **barks**; the slaves **rush in** and **arrest** the thief.*

A historical present in Latin can be translated *either* by an English present tense (as in the example above) *or* by a past tense.

---

*The endings of each tense are listed in the standard order, i.e. 1st, 2nd, and 3rd person singular endings, followed by 1st, 2nd, and 3rd person plural.

4   The present tense is also used to indicate an action which has begun earlier and is still going on; it is usually translated by an English perfect tense:

trēs hōrās eum *exspectō!*   *I have been waiting for him for three hours!*

5

first conjugation	second conjugation	third conjugation	third "-iō" conjugation	fourth conjugation
PERFECT *(I have carried, I carried, etc.)*				
port*āvī*	**docu***ī*	**trāx***ī*	**cēp***ī*	**aud***īvī*
port*āvistī*	**docu***istī*	**trāx***istī*	**cēp***istī*	**aud***īvistī*
port*āvit*	**docu***it*	**trāx***it*	**cēp***it*	**aud***īvit*
port*āvimus*	**docu***imus*	**trāx***imus*	**cēp***imus*	**aud***īvimus*
port*āvistis*	**docu***istis*	**trāx***istis*	**cēp***istis*	**aud***īvistis*
port*āvērunt*	**docu***ērunt*	**trāx***ērunt*	**cēp***ērunt*	**aud***īvērunt*
FUTURE PERFECT *(I shall/will have carried, etc.; but usually translated by an English present or perfect tense)*				
port*āverō*	**docu***erō*	**trāx***erō*	**cēp***erō*	**aud***īverō*
port*āveris*	**docu***eris*	**trāx***eris*	**cēp***eris*	**aud***īveris*
port*āverit*	**docu***erit*	**trāx***erit*	**cēp***erit*	**aud***īverit*
port*āverimus*	**docu***erimus*	**trāx***erimus*	**cēp***erimus*	**aud***īverimus*
port*āveritis*	**docu***eritis*	**trāx***eritis*	**cēp***eritis*	**aud***īveritis*
port*āverint*	**docu***erint*	**trāx***erint*	**cēp***erint*	**aud***īverint*
PLUPERFECT *(I had carried, etc.)*				
port*āveram*	**docu***eram*	**trāx***eram*	**cēp***eram*	**aud***īveram*
port*āverās*	**docu***erās*	**trāx***erās*	**cēp***erās*	**aud***īverās*
port*āverat*	**docu***erat*	**trāx***erat*	**cēp***erat*	**aud***īverat*
port*āverāmus*	**docu***erāmus*	**trāx***erāmus*	**cēp***erāmus*	**aud***īverāmus*
port*āverātis*	**docu***erātis*	**trāx***erātis*	**cēp***erātis*	**aud***īverātis*
port*āverant*	**docu***erant*	**trāx***erant*	**cēp***erant*	**aud***īverant*

6   The 3rd person plural form of the perfect tense sometimes ends in **-ēre** instead of **-ērunt**:

portāvēre = **portāvērunt** = *they (have) carried*
trāxēre = **trāxērunt** = *they (have) dragged*

Further examples: audīvēre; salūtāvēre; discessēre; monuēre.
This way of forming the 3rd person plural of the perfect is especially common in poetry.

7   1st-conjugation verbs whose perfect tense is normally formed with the letter **-v-** sometimes shorten the endings of their perfect, future perfect, and pluperfect tenses. For example:

portāstī = **portāvistī** = *you (have) carried*
laudārat = **laudāverat** = *he had praised*

4th-conjugation verbs sometimes omit **-v-** in their perfect, future perfect, and pluperfect tenses. For example:

audiī = **audīvī** = *I (have) heard*

29

8   The future perfect tense is usually translated by an English present or perfect tense, to suit the sense of the sentence in which it occurs:

sī mē *rogāverit,* **respondēbō.**   *If he asks me, I'll reply.*
cum eum *vīderis,* **redī.**   *When you have seen him, come back.*

7c Indicative Passive

1

PRESENT *(I am carried, I am being carried, etc.)*

port*or*	doce*or*	trah*or*	cap*ior*	aud*ior*
port*āris*	doc*ēris*	trah*eris**	cap*eris*	aud*īris*
port*ātur*	doc*ētur*	trah*itur*	cap*itur*	aud*ītur*
port*āmur*	doc*ēmur*	trah*imur*	cap*imur*	aud*īmur*
port*āminī*	doc*ēminī*	trah*iminī*	cap*iminī*	aud*īminī*
port*antur*	doc*entur*	trah*untur*	cap*iuntur*	aud*iuntur*

FUTURE *(I shall/will be carried, etc.)*

port*ābor*	doc*ēbor*	trah*ar*	cap*iar*	aud*iar*
port*āberis*	doc*ēberis*	trah*ēris**	cap*iēris*	aud*iēris*
port*ābitur*	doc*ēbitur*	trah*ētur*	cap*iētur*	aud*iētur*
port*ābimur*	doc*ēbimur*	trah*ēmur*	cap*iēmur*	aud*iēmur*
port*ābiminī*	doc*ēbiminī*	trah*ēminī*	cap*iēminī*	aud*iēminī*
port*ābuntur*	doc*ēbuntur*	trah*entur*	cap*ientur*	aud*ientur*

IMPERFECT *(I was being carried, I used to be carried, etc.)*

port*ābar*	doc*ēbar*	trah*ēbar*	cap*iēbar*	aud*iēbar*
port*ābāris*	doc*ēbāris*	trah*ēbāris*	cap*iēbāris*	aud*iēbāris*
port*ābātur*	doc*ēbātur*	trah*ēbātur*	cap*iēbātur*	aud*iēbātur*
port*ābāmur*	doc*ēbāmur*	trah*ēbāmur*	cap*iēbāmur*	aud*iēbāmur*
port*ābāminī*	doc*ēbāminī*	trah*ēbāminī*	cap*iēbāminī*	aud*iēbāminī*
port*ābantur*	doc*ēbantur*	trah*ēbantur*	cap*iēbantur*	aud*iēbantur*

> The 2nd person singular form of the future and imperfect tenses of the passive sometimes ends in **-re** instead of **-ris**:
>
> **docēbere** = **docēberis** = *you will be taught*
> **audiēre** = **audiēris** = *you will be heard*
> **trahēbāre** = **trahēbāris** = *you were being dragged*

2

PERFECT *(I have been carried, I was carried, etc.)*

portātus *sum*	doctus *sum*	tractus *sum*	captus *sum*	audītus *sum*
portātus *es*	doctus *es*	tractus *es*	captus *es*	audītus *es*
portātus *est*	doctus *est*	tractus *est*	captus *est*	audītus *est*
portātī *sumus*	doctī *sumus*	tractī *sumus*	captī *sumus*	audītī *sumus*
portātī *estis*	doctī *estis*	tractī *estis*	captī *estis*	audītī *estis*
portātī *sunt*	doctī *sunt*	tractī *sunt*	captī *sunt*	audītī *sunt*

*Compare the pronunciation of **traheris** *you are being dragged* and **trahēris** *you will be dragged*.

FUTURE PERFECT *(I shall/will have been carried, etc., but usually translated by an English present or perfect tense)*

portātus erō	**doctus erō**	**tractus erō**	**captus erō**	**audītus erō**
portātus eris	**doctus eris**	**tractus eris**	**captus eris**	**audītus eris**
portātus erit	**doctus erit**	**tractus erit**	**captus erit**	**audītus erit**
portātī erimus	**doctī erimus**	**tractī erimus**	**captī erimus**	**audītī erimus**
portātī eritis	**doctī eritis**	**tractī eritis**	**captī eritis**	**audītī eritis**
portātī erunt	**doctī erunt**	**tractī erunt**	**captī erunt**	**audītī erunt**

PLUPERFECT *(I had been carried, etc.)*

portātus eram	**doctus eram**	**tractus eram**	**captus eram**	**audītus eram**
portātus erās	**doctus erās**	**tractus erās**	**captus erās**	**audītus erās**
portātus erat	**doctus erat**	**tractus erat**	**captus erat**	**audītus erat**
portātī erāmus	**doctī erāmus**	**tractī erāmus**	**captī erāmus**	**audītī erāmus**
portātī erātis	**doctī erātis**	**tractī erātis**	**captī erātis**	**audītī erātis**
portātī erant	**doctī erant**	**tractī erant**	**captī erant**	**audītī erant**

3 The tenses in paragraph 2 are formed with perfect passive participles, which change their endings to indicate number and gender. For example:

audītus est.	*He was heard.*
audīta est.	*She was heard.*
audītum est.	*It was heard.*
audītī sunt.	*They (masc.) were heard.*
audītae sunt.	*They (fem.) were heard.*
audīta sunt.	*They (neut.) were heard.*

4 *Exercise* With the help (if necessary) of **7b** and paragraphs 1 and 2 opposite, translate:

1 audīveram.
2 portābāmus.
3 docēs.
4 docēbunt.
5 trāxit.
6 capiētis.
7 trahor.
8 portātī sunt.
9 audiēbāminī.
10 captī erāmus.

In **7b** and paragraphs 1 and 2, find the Latin for:

11 He captures.
12 They will drag.
13 We have been carried.
14 You (sg.) were being taught.
15 I shall have been heard.
16 He was hearing.
17 You (pl.) will be taught.
18 We drag.
19 I had been carried.
20 You (pl.) have captured.

7d Subjunctive Active

1

first conjugation	second conjugation	third conjugation	third "-iō" conjugation	fourth conjugation
PRESENT				
portem	**doceam**	**traham**	**capiam**	**audiam**
portēs	**doceās**	**trahās**	**capiās**	**audiās**
portet	**doceat**	**trahat**	**capiat**	**audiat**
portēmus	**doceāmus**	**trahāmus**	**capiāmus**	**audiāmus**
portētis	**doceātis**	**trahātis**	**capiātis**	**audiātis**
portent	**doceant**	**trahant**	**capiant**	**audiant**
IMPERFECT				
portārem	**docērem**	**traherem**	**caperem**	**audīrem**
portārēs	**docērēs**	**traherēs**	**caperēs**	**audīrēs**
portāret	**docēret**	**traheret**	**caperet**	**audīret**
portārēmus	**docērēmus**	**traherēmus**	**caperēmus**	**audīrēmus**
portārētis	**docērētis**	**traherētis**	**caperētis**	**audīrētis**
portārent	**docērent**	**traherent**	**caperent**	**audīrent**
PERFECT				
portāverim	**docuerim**	**trāxerim**	**cēperim**	**audīverim**
portāverīs	**docuerīs**	**trāxerīs**	**cēperīs**	**audīverīs**
portāverit	**docuerit**	**trāxerit**	**cēperit**	**audīverit**
portāverīmus	**docuerīmus**	**trāxerīmus**	**cēperīmus**	**audīverīmus**
portāverītis	**docuerītis**	**trāxerītis**	**cēperītis**	**audīverītis**
portāverint	**docuerint**	**trāxerint**	**cēperint**	**audīverint**
PLUPERFECT				
portāvissem	**docuissem**	**trāxissem**	**cēpissem**	**audīvissem**
portāvissēs	**docuissēs**	**trāxissēs**	**cēpissēs**	**audīvissēs**
portāvisset	**docuisset**	**trāxisset**	**cēpisset**	**audīvisset**
portāvissēmus	**docuissēmus**	**trāxissēmus**	**cēpissēmus**	**audīvissēmus**
portāvissētis	**docuissētis**	**trāxissētis**	**cēpissētis**	**audīvissētis**
portāvissent	**docuissent**	**trāxissent**	**cēpissent**	**audīvissent**

2   For examples of ways in which the subjunctive is used, see **35**.1–2.

3   There are many different ways of translating the subjunctive, especially in the present and imperfect tenses; the correct translation always depends on the way the subjunctive is being used in the sentence. The perfect and pluperfect subjunctive tenses, e.g. **portāverim** and **audīvissem**, are usually (but not always) translated in the same way as the perfect and pluperfect indicative, e.g. *I have carried, I had heard*, etc.

4   The subjunctive has no future or future perfect tenses. Instead, the future participle is used with the present or imperfect subjunctive of **sum** *I am*:

   nesciunt quandō amīcus tuus *adventūrus sit.*
   *They do not know when your friend **is going to arrive**.*
   Or, *They do not know when your friend **will arrive**.*

   in animō volvēbam quid *vīsūrus essem.*
   *I was wondering what **I was going to see**.*
   Or, *I was wondering what **I would see**.*

5   Some verbs (see **7b**.7) can shorten the forms of their perfect and pluperfect subjunctive tenses. For example:

   audierit = audīverit   portāssem = portāvissem

7e Subjunctive Passive

PRESENT

port*er*	doce*ar*	trah*ar*	capi*ar*	audi*ar*
port*ēris*	doce*āris*	trah*āris*	capi*āris*	audi*āris*
port*ētur*	doce*ātur*	trah*ātur*	capi*ātur*	audi*ātur*
port*ēmur*	doce*āmur*	trah*āmur*	capi*āmur*	audi*āmur*
port*ēminī*	doce*āminī*	trah*āminī*	capi*āminī*	audi*āminī*
port*entur*	doce*antur*	trah*antur*	capi*antur*	audi*antur*

IMPERFECT

port*ārer*	doc*ērer*	trah*erer*	cap*erer*	aud*īrer*
port*ārēris*	doc*ērēris*	trah*erēris*	cap*erēris*	aud*īrēris*
port*ārētur*	doc*ērētur*	trah*erētur*	cap*erētur*	aud*īrētur*
port*ārēmur*	doc*ērēmur*	trah*erēmur*	cap*erēmur*	aud*īrēmur*
port*ārēminī*	doc*ērēminī*	trah*erēminī*	cap*erēminī*	aud*īrēminī*
port*ārentur*	doc*ērentur*	trah*erentur*	cap*erentur*	aud*īrentur*

PERFECT

port*ātus sim*	doct*us sim*	tract*us sim*	capt*us sim*	audīt*us sim*
port*ātus sīs*	doct*us sīs*	tract*us sīs*	capt*us sīs*	audīt*us sīs*
port*ātus sit*	doct*us sit*	tract*us sit*	capt*us sit*	audīt*us sit*
port*ātī sīmus*	doct*ī sīmus*	tract*ī sīmus*	capt*ī sīmus*	audīt*ī sīmus*
port*ātī sītis*	doct*ī sītis*	tract*ī sītis*	capt*ī sītis*	audīt*ī sītis*
port*ātī sint*	doct*ī sint*	tract*ī sint*	capt*ī sint*	audīt*ī sint*

PLUPERFECT

port*ātus essem*	doct*us essem*	tract*us essem*	capt*us essem*	audīt*us essem*
port*ātus essēs*	doct*us essēs*	tract*us essēs*	capt*us essēs*	audīt*us essēs*
port*ātus esset*	doct*us esset*	tract*us esset*	capt*us esset*	audīt*us esset*
port*ātī essēmus*	doct*ī essēmus*	tract*ī essēmus*	capt*ī essēmus*	audīt*ī essēmus*
port*ātī essētis*	doct*ī essētis*	tract*ī essētis*	capt*ī essētis*	audīt*ī essētis*
port*ātī essent*	doct*ī essent*	tract*ī essent*	capt*ī essent*	audīt*ī essent*

> The 2nd person singular form of the present and imperfect tenses of the subjunctive passive sometimes ends in **-re** instead of **-ris**:
>
> PRESENT: **portēre** = **portēris**,   **doceāre** = **doceāris**, etc.
> IMPERFECT: **portārēre** = **portārēris**, **docērēre** = **docērēris**, etc.

7f Other Forms of the Verb

1   IMPERATIVE ACTIVE *(Carry!, etc.)*

*singular**	**portā**	**docē**	**trahe**	**cape**	**audī**
plural	**portāte**	**docēte**	**trahite**	**capite**	**audīte**

---

* The verbs **dīcō**, **dūcō**, and **faciō** have a short form of the imperative singular: **dīc!** *Say! Tell!*, **dūc!** *Lead! Take!*, and **fac!** *Do! Make!*

2 IMPERATIVE PASSIVE *(Be carried!, etc.)*

singular	**portāre**	**docēre**	**trahere**	**capere**	**audīre**
plural	**portāminī**	**docēminī**	**trahiminī**	**capiminī**	**audīminī**

3 PRESENT PARTICIPLE *(carrying, etc.)*
Present participles change their endings the same way as **ingēns** (shown in **2**.2):

SINGULAR					
nominative and vocative	**portāns**	**docēns**	**trahēns**	**capiēns**	**audiēns**
genitive	**portantis**	**docentis**	**trehentis**	**capientis**	**audientis**
dative	**portantī**	**docentī**	**trahentī**	**capientī**	**audientī**
accusative	**portantem**	**docentem**	**trahentem**	**capientem**	**audientem**
ablative	**portant-ī/-e**	**docent-ī/-e**	**trahent-ī/-e**	**capient-ī/-e**	**audient-ī/-e**
PLURAL					
nominative and vocative	**portantēs**	**docentēs**	**trahentēs**	**capientēs**	**audientēs**
genitive	**portantium**	**docentium**	**trahentium**	**capientium**	**audientium**
dative	**portantibus**	**docentibus**	**trahentibus**	**capientibus**	**audientibus**
accusative	**portantēs**	**docentēs**	**trahentēs**	**capientēs**	**audientēs**
ablative	**portantibus**	**docentibus**	**trahentibus**	**capientibus**	**audientibus**

Participles used as adjectives (cf. **2**.2, note under **ingēns**) usually have an **-ī** ending in the ablative singular when they modify a stated noun, e.g. **ā puerō dormientī** *by the sleeping boy;* they usually have an **-e** ending when they are used in ablative absolutes, e.g. **puerō dormiente** *while the boy sleeps.*

4 PERFECT PASSIVE PARTICIPLE *(having been carried, etc.)*

singular	**portātus**	**doctus**	**tractus**	**captus**	**audītus**
plural	**portātī**	**doctī**	**tractī**	**captī**	**audītī**

Perfect passive participles change their endings the same way as **bonus** (shown in **2**.1).

> For perfect active participles, see Deponent Verbs, **8c**.3.

5 FUTURE PARTICIPLE *(about to carry, etc.)*

singular	**portātūrus**	**doctūrus**	**tractūrus**	**captūrus**	**audītūrus**
plural	**portātūrī**	**doctūrī**	**tractūrī**	**captūrī**	**audītūrī**

Future Participles change their endings the same way as **bonus** (shown in **2**.1).

> For examples of ways in which participles are used, see **20**.1–10.

6 PRESENT ACTIVE INFINITIVE *(to carry, etc.)*

portāre	**docēre**	**trahere**	**capere**	**audīre**

7 PRESENT PASSIVE INFINITIVE *(to be carried, etc.)*
   portārī   docērī   trahī   capī   audīrī

8 PERFECT ACTIVE INFINITIVE *(to have carried, etc.)*
   portāvisse docuisse   trāxisse   cēpisse   audīvisse
   sometimes **portāsse**   *sometimes* **audīsse**

9 PERFECT PASSIVE INFINITIVE *(to have been carried, etc.)*
   portātus esse doctus esse   tractus esse   captus esse   audītus esse

   portātus in **portātus esse**, **doctus** in **doctus esse**, etc. change their
   endings to agree with the nouns they refer to, e.g. **crēdunt āram**
   ***captam esse**. They believe that the **altar has been captured**.*

10 FUTURE ACTIVE INFINITIVE *(to be about to carry, etc.)*
    portātūrus esse doctūrus esse tractūrus esse captūrus esse audītūrus esse

    portātūrus in **portātūrus esse**, **doctūrus** in **doctūrus esse**, etc. change
    their endings to agree with the nouns they refer to, e.g. **spērāvit eōs**
    frūmentum *portātūrōs esse. He hoped that **they would carry** the grain.*

11 FUTURE PASSIVE INFINITIVE *(to be about to be carried, etc.)*
    portātum īrī   doctum īrī   tractum īrī   captum īrī   audītum īrī

    The endings of **portātum** in **portātum īrī**, **doctum** in **doctum īrī**, etc. do
    not change.

    For examples of ways in which infinitives are used, see **21.1–8** and **25.4**.

12 GERUND *(carrying, etc.)*
    nominative (no forms)

genitive	**portandī**	**docendī**	**trahendī**	**capiendī**	**audiendī**
dative	**portandō**	**docendō**	**trahendō**	**capiendō**	**audiendō**
accusative	**portandum**	**docendum**	**trahendum**	**capiendum**	**audiendum**
ablative	**portandō**	**docendō**	**trahendō**	**capiendō**	**audiendō**

    The gerund has no nominative or plural forms.

13 GERUNDIVE *(being carried, needing to be carried, etc.)*
    portandus docendus   trahendus   capiendus   audiendus

    Gerundives change their endings in the same way as **bonus** (shown in
    2.1).

14 SUPINE (for translation, see **26.3**)

accusative	**portātum**	**doctum**	**tractum**	**captum**	**audītum**
ablative	**portātū**	**doctū**	**tractū**	**captū**	**audītū**

    For examples of ways in which the gerund, gerundive, and supine are
    used, see **26.1–3**.

8 Deponent Verbs

(i.e. verbs which have passive forms and active meanings)

8a Indicative forms of

cōnor	*I try*	**patior**	*I suffer*	
vereor	*I fear*	**mentior**	*I lie, I tell a lie*	
loquor	*I speak*			

1

first conjugation	*second conjugation*	*third conjugation*	*third "-iō" conjugation*	*fourth conjugation*
PRESENT *(I try, I am trying, etc.)*				
cōnor	**vere**or	**loqu**or	**pati**or	**menti**or
cōnāris	**ver**ēris	**loqu**eris	**pat**eris	**ment**īris
cōnātur	**ver**ētur	**loqu**itur	**pat**itur	**ment**ītur
cōnāmur	**ver**ēmur	**loqu**imur	**pat**imur	**ment**īmur
cōnāminī	**ver**ēminī	**loqu**iminī	**pat**iminī	**ment**īminī
cōnantur	**ver**entur	**loqu**untur	**pat**iuntur	**ment**iuntur
FUTURE *(I shall/I will try, etc.)*				
cōnābor	**ver**ēbor	**loqu**ar	**pati**ar	**menti**ar
cōnāberis	**ver**ēberis	**loqu**ēris	**pati**ēris	**menti**ēris
cōnābitur	**ver**ēbitur	**loqu**ētur	**pati**ētur	**menti**ētur
cōnābimur	**ver**ēbimur	**loqu**ēmur	**pati**ēmur	**menti**ēmur
cōnābiminī	**ver**ēbiminī	**loqu**ēminī	**pati**ēminī	**menti**ēminī
cōnābuntur	**ver**ēbuntur	**loqu**entur	**pati**entur	**menti**entur
IMPERFECT *(I was trying, I used to try, etc.)*				
cōnābar	**ver**ēbar	**loqu**ēbar	**pati**ēbar	**menti**ēbar
cōnābāris	**ver**ēbāris	**loqu**ēbāris	**pati**ēbāris	**menti**ēbāris
cōnābātur	**ver**ēbātur	**loqu**ēbātur	**pati**ēbātur	**menti**ēbātur
cōnābāmur	**ver**ēbāmur	**loqu**ēbāmur	**pati**ēbāmur	**menti**ēbāmur
cōnābāminī	**ver**ēbāminī	**loqu**ēbāminī	**pati**ēbāminī	**menti**ēbāminī
cōnābantur	**ver**ēbantur	**loqu**ēbantur	**pati**ēbantur	**menti**ēbantur

Compare these and other forms of **cōnor, vereor, loquor, patior,** and **mentior** with the PASSIVE forms of **portō, doceō, trahō, capiō,** and **audiō** (shown in **7c.1–2, 7e,** and **7f**).

2   **patior** belongs to a group of deponent verbs which form some of their endings like third-conjugation verbs such as **loquor** but form other endings (italicized) like fourth-conjugation verbs such as **mentior**. Other common verbs in this group are **gradior** and its compounds (e.g. **ēgredior, ingredior,** and other verbs listed in **36.4e**) and **morior**.

PERFECT *(I have tried, I tried, etc.)*

cōnātus sum	veritus sum	locūtus sum	passus sum	mentītus sum
cōnātus es	veritus es	locūtus es	passus es	mentītus es
cōnātus est	veritus est	locūtus est	passus est	mentītus est
cōnātī sumus	veritī sumus	locūtī sumus	passī sumus	mentītī sumus
cōnātī estis	veritī estis	locūtī estis	passī estis	mentītī estis
cōnātī sunt	veritī sunt	locūtī sunt	passī sunt	mentītī sunt

FUTURE PERFECT *(I shall/will have tried, etc., but usually translated by an English present or perfect tense)*

cōnātus erō	veritus erō	locūtus erō	passus erō	mentītus erō
cōnātus eris	veritus eris	locūtus eris	passus eris	mentītus eris
cōnātus erit	veritus erit	locūtus erit	passus erit	mentītus erit
cōnātī erimus	veritī erimus	locūtī erimus	passī erimus	mentītī erimus
cōnātī eritis	veritī eritis	locūtī eritis	passī eritis	mentītī eritis
cōnātī erunt	veritī erunt	locūtī erunt	passī erunt	mentītī erunt

PLUPERFECT *(I had tried, etc.)*

cōnātus eram	veritus eram	locūtus eram	passus eram	mentītus eram
cōnātus erās	veritus erās	locūtus erās	passus erās	mentītus erās
cōnātus erat	veritus erat	locūtus erat	passus erat	mentītus erat
cōnātī erāmus	veritī erāmus	locūtī erāmus	passī erāmus	mentītī erāmus
cōnātī erātis	veritī erātis	locūtī erātis	passī erātis	mentītī erātis
cōnātī erant	veritī erant	locūtī erant	passī erant	mentītī erant

3 *Exercise*   With the help (if necessary) of paragraphs 1 and 2 opposite, translate:

1 cōnābantur.   4 veritus est.
2 locūtus eram.   5 mentiēmur.
3 patiminī.   6 verēbitur.

In paragraphs 1 and 2, find the Latin for:

7 We try.   10 You (sg.) had feared.
8 I have suffered.   11 He will suffer.
9 You (pl.) were speaking.   12 They told lies.

8b Subjunctive

PRESENT

cōner	verear	loquar	patiar	mentiar
cōnēris	vereāris	loquāris	patiāris	mentiāris
cōnētur	vereātur	loquātur	patiātur	mentiātur
cōnēmur	vereāmur	loquāmur	patiāmur	mentiāmur
cōnēminī	vereāminī	loquāminī	patiāminī	mentiāminī
cōnentur	vereantur	loquantur	patiantur	mentiantur

IMPERFECT

cōnārer	verērer	loquerer	paterer	mentīrer
cōnārēris	verērēris	loquerēris	paterēris	mentīrēris
cōnārētur	verērētur	loquerētur	paterētur	mentīrētur
cōnārēmur	verērēmur	loquerēmur	paterēmur	mentīrēmur
cōnārēminī	verērēminī	loquerēminī	paterēminī	mentīrēminī
cōnārentur	verērentur	loquerentur	paterentur	mentīrentur

PERFECT

cōnātus sim	veritus sim	locūtus sim	passus sim	mentītus sim
cōnātus sīs	veritus sīs	locūtus sīs	passus sīs	mentītus sis
cōnātus sit	veritus sit	locūtus sit	passus sit	mentītus sit
cōnātī sīmus	veritī sīmus	locūtī sīmus	passī sīmus	mentītī sīmus
cōnātī sītis	veritī sītis	locūtī sītis	passī sītis	mentītī sītis
cōnātī sint	veritī sint	locūtī sint	passī sint	mentītī sint

PLUPERFECT

cōnātus essem	veritus essem	locūtus essem	passus essem	mentītus essem
cōnātus essēs	veritus essēs	locūtus essēs	passus essēs	mentītus essēs
cōnātus esset	veritus esset	locūtus esset	passus esset	mentītus esset
cōnātī essēmus	veritī essēmus	locūtī essēmus	passī essēmus	mentītī essēmus
cōnātī essētis	veritī essētis	locūtī essētis	passī essētis	mentītī essētis
cōnātī essent	veritī essent	locūtī essent	passī essent	mentītī essent

8c Other Forms

1 IMPERATIVE *(Try!, Fear!, etc.)*

singular	**cōnāre**	**verēre**	**loquere**	**patere**	**mentīre**
plural	**cōnāminī**	**verēminī**	**loquiminī**	**patiminī**	**mentīminī**

2 PRESENT PARTICIPLE *(trying, fearing, etc.)*

SINGULAR

nominative and vocative	**cōnāns**	**verēns**	**loquēns**	**patiēns**	**mentiēns**
genitive	**cōnantis**	**verentis**	**loquentis**	**patientis**	**mentientis**
dative	**cōnantī**	**verentī**	**loquentī**	**patientī**	**mentientī**
accusative	**cōnantem**	**verentem**	**loquentem**	**patientem**	**mentientem**
ablative	**cōnant-ī/-e**	**verent-ī/-e**	**loquent-ī/-e**	**patient-ī/-e**	**mentient-ī/-e**

PLURAL

nominative and vocative	**cōnantēs**	**verentēs**	**loquentēs**	**patientēs**	**mentientēs**
genitive	**cōnantium**	**verentium**	**loquentium**	**patientium**	**mentientium**
dative	**cōnantibus**	**verentibus**	**loquentibus**	**patientibus**	**mentientibus**
accusative	**cōnantēs**	**verentēs**	**loquentēs**	**patientēs**	**mentientēs**
ablative	**cōnantibus**	**verentibus**	**loquentibus**	**patientibus**	**mentientibus**

For uses of the alternative endings of the ablative singular, see **7f**.3.

3 PERFECT ACTIVE PARTICIPLE *(having tried, etc.)*

singular	**cōnātus**	**veritus**	**locūtus**	**passus**	**mentītus**
plural	**cōnātī**	**veritī**	**locūtī**	**passī**	**mentītī**

Perfect active participles change their endings the same way as **bonus** (shown in **2**.1).

4 FUTURE PARTICIPLE *(about to try, about to fear, etc.)*

singular	**cōnātūrus**	**veritūrus**	**locūtūrus**	**passūrus**	**mentītūrus**
plural	**cōnātūrī**	**veritūrī**	**locūtūrī**	**passūrī**	**mentītūrī**

Future participles change their endings the same way as **bonus** (shown in **2**.1).

5 PRESENT INFINITIVE *(to try, to fear, etc.)*

cōnārī	**verērī**	**loquī**	**patī**	**mentīrī**

6 PERFECT INFINITIVE *(to have tried, etc.)*

cōnātus esse	**veritus esse**	**locūtus esse**	**passus esse**	**mentītus esse**

For the changing endings of **cōnātus** in **cōnātus esse**, etc., cf. **7f**.9.

7 FUTURE INFINITIVE *(to be about to try, etc.)*

cōnātūrus esse	**veritūrus esse**	**locūtūrus esse**	**passūrus esse**	**mentītūrus esse**

For the changing endings of **cōnātūrus** in **cōnātūrus esse**, etc., cf. **7f**.10.

8   GERUND *(trying, fearing, etc.)*
   nominative (no forms)

genitive	**cōnandī**	**verendī**	**loquendī**	**patiendī**	**mentiendī**
dative	**cōnandō**	**verendō**	**loquendō**	**patiendō**	**mentiendō**
accusative	**cōnandum**	**verendum**	**loquendum**	**patiendum**	**mentiendum**
ablative	**cōnandō**	**verendō**	**loquendō**	**patiendō**	**mentiendō**

The gerund has no nominative or plural forms.

9   GERUNDIVE *(for translation, see* **26**.2)

   cōnandus   verendus   loquendus   patiendus   mentiendus

Gerundives change their endings the same way as **bonus** (shown in **2**.1).

10   SUPINE (for translation, see **26**.3*)*

accusative	**cōnātum**	**veritum**	**locūtum**	**passum**	**mentītum**
ablative	**cōnātū**	**veritū**	**locūtū**	**passū**	**mentītū**

Deponent verbs normally have passive forms but active meanings. The only exceptions are the present and future participles, future infinitive, gerund, and supine, which have active forms (e.g. **cōnāns, cōnātūrus, cōnātūrus esse, cōnandum,** and **cōnātum**) and the gerundive, which has a passive meaning (e.g. **loquendus** *being spoken, needing to be spoken*).

8d Semi-Deponent Verbs

1   A few verbs, such as **audeō** *I dare*, are known as *semi-deponent verbs*, because they form their present, future, and imperfect tenses in the ordinary way, but form their perfect, future perfect, and pluperfect tenses like deponent verbs, i.e. with passive forms and active meanings. For example:

   Ordinary forms: **audeō** *I dare* **audēbō** *I shall/will dare* **audēbam** *I was daring*
   Deponent-like forms: **ausus sum** *I dared* **ausus erō** *I shall/will have dared*
   ausus eram *I had dared*

Other semi-deponent verbs are **cōnfīdō** *I trust*, **gaudeō** *I am glad*, and **soleō** *I am accustomed*. The principal parts of these verbs are:

audeō	**audēre**	**ausus sum**
cōnfīdō	**cōnfīdere**	**cōnfīsus sum**
gaudeō	**gaudēre**	**gāvīsus sum**
soleō	**solēre**	**solitus sum**

2   *Exercise* With the help of 1 above, translate:

   1 solēbant.   2 cōnfīsa est.   3 gāvīsī erant.   4 audēbunt.

9 Irregular Verbs

1	**sum**	*I am*	**volō**	*I want*		**ferō**	*I bring*
	possum	*I am able*	**nōlō**	*I do not want*		**fīō**	*I am made, I become*
	eō	*I go*	**mālō**	*I want more, I prefer*			

PRESENT *(I am, etc.)*

sum	possum	eō	volō	nōlō	mālō	ferō	fīō
es	potes	īs	vīs	nōn vīs	māvīs	fers	fīs
est	potest	it	vult	nōn vult	māvult	fert	fit
sumus	possumus	īmus	volumus	nōlumus	mālumus	ferimus	–
estis	potestis	ītis	vultis	nōn vultis	māvultis	fertis	–
sunt	possunt	eunt	volunt	nōlunt	mālunt	ferunt	fīunt

FUTURE *(I shall/I will be, etc.)*

erō	poterō	ībō	volam	nōlam	mālam	feram	fīam
eris	poteris	ībis	volēs	nōlēs	mālēs	ferēs	fīēs
erit	poterit	ībit	volet	nōlet	mālet	feret	fīet
erimus	poterimus	ībimus	volēmus	nōlēmus	mālēmus	ferēmus	fīēmus
eritis	poteritis	ībitis	volētis	nōlētis	mālētis	ferētis	fīētis
erunt	poterunt	ībunt	volent	nōlent	mālent	ferent	fīent

IMPERFECT *(I was, etc.)*

eram	poteram	ībam	volēbam	nōlēbam	mālēbam	ferēbam	fīēbam
erās	poterās	ībās	volēbās	nōlēbās	mālēbās	ferēbās	fīēbās
erat	poterat	ībat	volēbat	nōlēbat	mālēbat	ferēbat	fīēbat
erāmus	poterāmus	ībāmus	volēbāmus	nōlēbāmus	mālēbāmus	ferēbāmus	fīēbāmus
erātis	poterātis	ībātis	volēbātis	nōlēbātis	mālēbātis	ferēbātis	fīēbātis
erant	poterant	ībant	volēbant	nōlēbant	mālēbant	ferēbant	fīēbant

PERFECT *(I have been or I was, etc.)*

fuī	potuī	iī	voluī	nōluī	māluī	tulī	factus sum*
fuistī	potuistī	iistī	voluistī	nōluistī	māluistī	tulistī	factus es
fuit	potuit	iit	voluit	nōluit	māluit	tulit	factus est
fuimus	potuimus	iimus	voluimus	nōluimus	māluimus	tulimus	factī sumus
fuistis	potuistis	iistis	voluistis	nōluistis	māluistis	tulistis	factī estis
fuērunt	potuērunt	iērunt	voluērunt	nōluērunt	māluērunt	tulērunt	factī sunt

FUTURE PERFECT *(I shall/will have been, etc.)*

fuerō	potuerō	ierō	voluerō	nōluerō	māluerō	tulerō	factus erō*
fueris	potueris	ieris	volueris	nōlueris	mālueris	tuleris	factus eris
fuerit	potuerit	ierit	voluerit	nōluerit	māluerit	tulerit	factus erit
fuerimus	potuerimus	ierimus	voluerimus	nōluerimus	māluerimus	tulerimus	factī erimus
fueritis	potueritis	ieritis	volueritis	nōlueritis	mālueritis	tuleritis	factī eritis
fuerint	potuerint	ierint	voluerint	nōluerint	māluerint	tulerint	factī erunt

*For these tenses of **fīō**, passive forms of **faciō** are used, e.g. **factus sum** *I was made, I became.*

PLUPERFECT *(I had been, etc.)*

fueram	potueram	ieram	volueram	nōlueram	mālueram	tuleram	factus eram*
fuerās	potuerās	ierās	voluerās	nōluerās	māluerās	tulerās	factus erās
fuerat	potuerat	ierat	voluerat	nōluerat	māluerat	tulerat	factus erat
fuerāmus	potuerāmus	ierāmus	voluerāmus	nōluerāmus	māluerāmus	tulerāmus	factī erāmus
fuerātis	potuerātis	ierātis	voluerātis	nōluerātis	māluerātis	tulerātis	factī erātis
fuerant	potuerant	ierant	voluerant	nōluerant	māluerant	tulerant	factī erant

2 *Subjunctive*

PRESENT SUBJUNCTIVE

sim	possim	eam	velim	nōlim	mālim	feram	fīam
sīs	possīs	eās	velīs	nōlīs	mālīs	ferās	fīās
sit	possit	eat	velit	nōlit	mālit	ferat	fīat
sīmus	possīmus	eāmus	velīmus	nōlīmus	mālīmus	ferāmus	fīāmus
sītis	possītis	eātis	velītis	nōlītis	mālītis	ferātis	fīātis
sint	possint	eant	velint	nōlint	mālint	ferant	fīant

IMPERFECT SUBJUNCTIVE

essem**	possem	īrem	vellem	nōllem	māllem	ferrem	fierem
essēs	possēs	īrēs	vellēs	nōllēs	māllēs	ferrēs	fierēs
esset	posset	īret	vellet	nōllet	māllet	ferret	fieret
essēmus	possēmus	īrēmus	vellēmus	nōllēmus	māllēmus	ferrēmus	fierēmus
essētis	possētis	īrētis	vellētis	nōllētis	māllētis	ferrētis	fierētis
essent	possent	īrent	vellent	nōllent	māllent	ferrent	fierent

PERFECT SUBJUNCTIVE

fuerim	potuerim	ierim	voluerim	nōluerim	māluerim	tulerim	factus sim†
fuerīs	potuerīs	ierīs	voluerīs	nōluerīs	māluerīs	tulerīs	factus sīs
fuerit	potuerit	ierit	voluerit	nōluerit	māluerit	tulerit	factus sit
fuerīmus	potuerīmus	ierīmus	voluerīmus	nōluerīmus	māluerīmus	tulerīmus	factī sīmus
fuerītis	potuerītis	ierītis	voluerītis	nōluerītis	māluerītis	tulerītis	factī sītis
fuerint	potuerint	ierint	voluerint	nōluerint	māluerint	tulerint	factī sint

PLUPERFECT SUBJUNCTIVE

fuissem	potuissem	iissem	voluissem	nōluissem	māluissem	tulissem	factus essem†
fuissēs	potuissēs	iissēs	voluissēs	nōluissēs	māluissēs	tulissēs	factus essēs
fuisset	potuisset	iisset	voluisset	nōluisset	māluisset	tulisset	factus esset
fuissēmus	potuissēmus	iissēmus	voluissēmus	nōluissēmus	māluissēmus	tulissēmus	factī essēmus
fuissētis	potuissētis	iissētis	voluissētis	nōluissētis	māluissētis	tulissētis	factī essētis
fuissent	potuissent	iissent	voluissent	nōluissent	māluissent	tulissent	factī essent

** Sometimes **forem, forēs, foret, forēmus, forētis, forent**.

†For these tenses of **fīam**, passive forms of **faciō** are used, e.g. **factus sim.**

3 Other Forms

IMPERATIVE SINGULAR AND PLURAL

| es, este | – | ī, īte | – | nōlī, nōlīte* | – | fer, ferte | fī, fīte |

PRESENT PARTICIPLE

| –** | potēns*** | iēns§ | volēns | nōlēns | – | ferēns | – |

FUTURE PARTICIPLE

| futūrus | – | itūrus | – | – | – | lātūrus | – |

PRESENT INFINITIVE

| esse | posse | īre | velle | nōlle | mālle | ferre | fierī |

PERFECT INFINITIVE

| fuisse | potuisse | iisse | voluisse | nōluisse | māluisse | tulisse | factus esse† |

FUTURE INFINITIVE

| futūrus esse –
sometimes **fore** | | itūrus esse – | – | – | – | lātūrus
esse | – |

GERUND

| – | – | eundum | volendum – | | – | ferendum– | |

SUPINE

| – | – | itum | – | – | – | lātum | – |

For passive forms of **ferō**, see paragraph 5.

4   The forms of **fīō** are used as present, future, and imperfect tenses of the passive of **faciō** *I make, I do*, etc.

> **servī nihil faciunt.** **nihil** *fit*.
> *The slaves are doing nothing.* *Nothing **is being done**.*
> Or, *Nothing **is happening**.*

> **populus mē rēgem faciet.** **rēx** *fiam*.
> *The people will make me king.* ***I shall be made** king.*
> Or, ***I shall become** king.*

---

*   For examples of **nōlī** and **nōlīte** used with an infinitive to order somebody not to do something (e.g. **nōlī dīcere!** *Don't speak!*), see **12**.2 and **21**.2.

**   **sum** has no present participle, but compounds of **sum**, such as **absum, praesum**, and the other verbs listed in **36**.6e, have present participles ending in -**ēns**, e.g. **absēns** *being away*, **praesēns** *being in charge*.

*** **potēns** is used as an adjective, meaning "powerful."

§   The present participle of **eō** is very rarely met, but compounds of **eō**, such as **exeō, redeō**, and the other verbs listed in **36**.6a, have present participles ending in -**iēns** (genitive -**euntis**), e.g. **exiēns** (genitive **exeuntis**) *going out*, **rediēns** (genitive **redeuntis**) *returning*.

†   For these forms, the passive of **faciō** is used, e.g. **factus esse** *to have been made, to have become*.

The other tenses of the passive of **faciō** are formed in the usual way:

equitēs impetum fēcērunt.   **impetus ab equitibus** *factus est.*
*The cavalry **made** an attack.*   *An attack **was made** by the cavalry.*

5   **ferō** has the following passive forms:

Indicative	Subjunctive
PRESENT *(I am brought)*	PRESENT
feror	**ferar**
ferris*	**ferāris**
fertur	**ferātur**
ferimur	**ferāmur**
feriminī	**ferāminī**
feruntur	**ferantur**
FUTURE *(I shall/will be brought)*	
ferar	
ferēris	
ferētur	
ferēmur	
ferēminī	
ferentur	
IMPERFECT *(I was being brought)*	IMPERFECT
ferēbar	**ferrer**
ferēbāris	**ferrēris**
ferēbātur	**ferrētur**
ferēbāmur	**ferrēmur**
ferēbāminī	**ferrēminī**
ferēbantur	**ferrentur**
PERFECT *(I have been brought, I was brought)*	PERFECT
lātus sum	**lātus sim**
lātus es	**lātus sīs**
lātus est	**lātus sit**
lātī sumus	**lātī sīmus**
lātī estis	**lātī sītis**
lātī sunt	**lātī sint**
FUTURE PERFECT *(I shall/will have been brought)*	
lātus erō	
lātus eris	
lātus erit	
lātī erimus	
lātī eritis	
lātī erunt	

*ferris is an extremely rare form; an alternate form, **fereris**, is also quite rare.

PLUPERFECT *(I had been brought)*	PLUPERFECT
lātus eram	**lātus essem**
lātus erās	**lātus essēs**
lātus erat	**lātus esset**
lātī erāmus	**lātī essēmus**
lātī erātis	**lātī essētis**
lātī erant	**lātī essent**

Other forms

IMPERATIVE *(Be carried!)*	PRESENT PASSIVE INFINITIVE *(to be brought)*
singular **ferre**	
plural **feriminī**	**ferrī**

PERFECT PASSIVE PARTICIPLE *(having been brought)*	PERFECT PASSIVE INFINITIVE *(to have been brought)*
lātus	**lātus esse**

GERUNDIVE *(being brought, needing to be brought)*	FUTURE PASSIVE INFINITIVE *(to be about to be brought)*
ferendus	**lātum īrī**

6 *Perfect Forms with Present Meanings*

nōvī *I know,* **ōdī** *I hate,* and **meminī** *I remember*

These verbs have three tenses whose meanings are present, future, and past, but whose endings are formed like the perfect, future perfect, and pluperfect of ordinary verbs:

Indicative

PERFECT WITH **PRESENT** MEANING *(I know, I hate, I remember, etc.)*

nōvī*	**ōdī**	**meminī**
nōvistī	**ōdistī**	**meministī**
nōvit	**ōdit**	**meminit**
nōvimus	**ōdimus**	**meminimus**
nōvistis	**ōdistis**	**meministis**
nōvērunt	**ōdērunt**	**meminērunt**

*****nōvī** *I have gotten to know,* therefore *I (now) know,* is the perfect tense of **nōscō** *I get to know, I am getting to know.*

FUTURE PERFECT WITH **FUTURE** MEANING *(I shall/will know, I shall/will hate, I shall/will remember, etc.)*

nōverō*	**ōderō**	**meminerō**
nōveris	**ōderis**	**memineris**
nōverit	**ōderit**	**meminerit**
nōverimus	**ōderimus**	**meminerimus**
nōveritis	**ōderitis**	**memineritis**
nōverint	**ōderint**	**meminerint**

* Alternative forms: **nōrō, nōris, nōrit, nōrimus, nōritis, nōrint**

PLUPERFECT WITH **PAST** MEANING *(I knew, I hated, I remembered, etc.)*

nōveram*	ōderam	memineram
nōverās	ōderās	meminerās
nōverat	ōderat	meminerat
nōverāmus	ōderāmus	meminerāmus
nōverātis	ōderātis	meminerātis
nōverant	ōderant	meminerant

*Alternative forms: **nōram, nōrās, nōrat, nōrāmus, nōrātis, nōrant**

Subjunctive

PERFECT WITH **PRESENT** MEANING

nōverim*	ōderim	meminerim
nōverīs	ōderīs	meminerīs
nōverit	ōderit	meminerit
nōverīmus	ōderīmus	meminerīmus
nōverītis	ōderītis	meminerītis
nōverint	ōderint	meminerint

*Alternative forms: **nōrim, nōrīs, nōrit, nōrīmus, nōrītis, nōrint**

PLUPERFECT WITH **PAST** MEANING

nōvissem*	ōdissem	meminissem
nōvissēs	ōdissēs	meminissēs
nōvisset	ōdisset	meminisset
nōvissēmus	ōdissēmus	meminissēmus
nōvissētis	ōdissētis	meminissētis
nōvissent	ōdissent	meminissent

*Alternative forms: **nōssem, nōssēs, nōsset, nōssēmus, nōssētis, nōssent**

Other Forms

INFINITIVE

nōvisse, nōsse	ōdisse	meminisse

IMPERATIVE, SINGULAR AND PLURAL

–	–	**mementō, mementōte**

FUTURE PARTICIPLE

–	**ōsūrus**	–

7 **coepī** *I have begun* or *I began*

coepī sometimes serves as the perfect for **incipiō** *I begin*, although **incēpī**, the true perfect of **incipiō**, also occurs. **coepī** also often means "I began."

Indicative	*Subjunctive*
PERFECT(*I have begun, I began*)	PERFECT
coepī	**coeperim**
coepistī	**coeperīs**
coepit	**coeperit**
coepimus	**coeperīmus**
coepistis	**coeperītis**
coepērunt	**coeperint**

INFINITIVE
coepisse *(to have begun)*

8 *Exercise* With the help of paragraphs 1–7, translate:

1 potest.	5 fuistī.	9 nōlumus.
2 ferimus.	6 fīēbant.	10 memineram.
3 ībunt.	7 lātus es.	11 nōvistis.
4 volēbātis.	8 ōderō.	12 māvultis.

In paragraphs 1–7, find the Latin for:

13 You (sg.) are.	17 We were going.
14 We go.	18 They were able.
15 He becomes.	19 I had been able.
16 You (pl.) want.	20 You (sg.) began.

With the help of paragraphs 1–7, work out the Latin for:

21 He has been.	22 You (pl.) were being brought.
23 They don't want (subjunctive).	24 They had become (subjunctive).

PART TWO

SYNTAX
(formation of sentences)

10 Statements

1 **currimus.**   *We run.*
  puerī dormiunt.   *The boys are asleep.*
  nōn manēbit.   *He (or she or it) will not stay.*
  spectātōrēs plausērunt, flōrēsque   *The spectators clapped and started*
    iactāre coepērunt.   *to throw flowers.*

2   Statements like those above are sometimes described as *direct* statements. For *indirect* statements, see **25**.4.

11 Questions

1 *introduced by a question-word,* such as **quis? quid? cūr? ubi?** etc.:

    quid **facitis?**   ***What** are you doing?*
    ubi **sunt leōnēs?**   ***Where** are the lions?*
    cūr **regrediēbantur?**   ***Why** were they going back?*

2 *with **-ne**,* added to the first word of the clause or sentence:

    audīvistī*ne* strepitum?   *Did you hear the din?*
    līberābitur*ne* captīvus?   *Will the prisoner be freed?*

3 *expressed by tone of voice,* indicated in writing by a question-mark:

    cibum habēs?   *Have you got food?*

4 *with **utrum** (sometimes omitted) followed by **an . . . ?** or **annōn?**,* to express alternatives:

    utrum **tē laudāvit *an* pūnīvit?**   *Did he praise you **or** punish you?*
    utrum **adhūc vīvit *annōn*?**   *Is he still alive **or not**?*
    canem *an* fēlem ēmistis?   *Did you buy a dog **or** a cat?*

5   *introduced by nōnne. . . ?*, to suggest that the answer to the question will be "yes":

    nōnne eum vīdistis?   ***Surely** you saw him?*
                                       Or, *You saw him, **didn't you?***

    nōnne rēx in aulā habitat?   ***Surely** the king lives in a palace?*
                                       Or, *The king lives in a palace, **doesn't he?***

6   *introduced by num. . . ?*, to suggest that the answer to the question will be "no":

    num servus es?   ***Surely** you aren't a slave?*
                                     Or, *You're **not** a slave, **are you?***

7   *with a subjunctive form of the verb*, indicating that the speaker is wondering what to do (*deliberative question*):

    ubi gemmās *cēlem?*   *Where **am I to hide** the jewels?*
    quōs deōs *precēmur?*   *Which gods **are we to pray to?***
    utrum *maneam* an *abeam?*   *Am I to stay or go away?*
    ānulum *reddāmus* an   *Should **we give** the ring **back** or*
        retineāmus?   *keep it?*

8   Further examples:

    1 labōrantne servī?
    2 īnsānus es an scelestus?
    3 nōnne puerī dormiēbant?
    4 quis tē sequēbātur?
    5 epistulam meam accēpistis?
    6 quandō advēnit nūntius?
    7 utrum aquam an vīnum bibitis?
    8 num oppidum captum est?
    9 cūr illum librum legis?
   10 fugiāmus an resistāmus?

> Questions like those in paragraphs 1–6 are sometimes described as *direct* questions, and those in paragraph 7 as *direct deliberative* questions. For *indirect* questions and *indirect deliberative* questions, see **25.2**.

12 Commands

1 *with an imperative form of the verb*, giving an order to somebody:
    trāde pecūniam!   *Hand over the money!*
    respondēte!   *Answer!*
    intrā!   *Come in!*
    mē *sequiminī!*   *Follow me!*
    cōnāre!   *Try!*

2 *with **nōlī** (plural **nōlīte**) and an infinitive*, ordering somebody NOT to do something:
    nōlī dormīre!   *Be unwilling to sleep!*
                     Or, in more natural English:
                      Don't sleep!

    nōlīte **mē** *dēserere!*   *Don't desert **me**!*
    nōlī respicere!   *Don't look back!*

3 *with a verb in the present tense of the subjunctive*, giving an order in the 1st person plural (and so including oneself in the order), or in the 3rd person singular or plural (and so giving an order *about* someone or something); this is known as the *jussive* use of the subjunctive:
    vīllam *ingrediāmur.*   *Let us go into the villa.*

    dīligentius *labōrent.*   *Let them work harder.*
                       Or, in more natural English:
                      They are to work harder.

    vīvāmus **atque** *amēmus.*   *Let us live and love.*

nē with the jussive subjunctive indicates that an order in the 1st or 3rd person is *negative*:
    nē dēspērēmus!   *Let us not despair!*
    nē haesitet **dominus.**   *Let the master **not** hesitate.*
                       Or, *The master **is not to hesitate**.*

> The jussive subjunctive is sometimes used in a 2nd-person form ("you" sg. or pl.) to indicate a mild command or piece of general advice:
>   **hūc** *reveniās.*   *You are to come back here.*
>   **parentibus** *pāreās.*   *You should obey your parents.*

4 Further examples:

1 accipe hanc pecūniam!   6 statim respondeāmus.
2 nōlīte currere!   7 nē in forō pugnēmus.
3 tacēte!   8 nūntius hodiē proficīscātur.
4 cavē canem!   9 loquere!
5 nōlī fundum vēndere!   10 cōnāminī!

5   Commands like those above are sometimes described as *direct* commands. For *indirect* commands, see **25**.3.

13 Wishes

1   *with **utinam** and the pluperfect subjunctive*, indicating a wish about the PAST (adding **nē** if the wish is negative):

       ***utinam** resistere potuissem!*   ***If only I had been able** to resist!*
                                          Or, *I **wish** I had been able to resist!*

       ***utinam nē** reversī essent!*   ***If only** they **had not** turned back!*

2   *with **utinam** and the imperfect subjunctive*, indicating a wish about the PRESENT (negative **nē**):

       ***utinam nē** in hōc carcere   I **wish** we **weren't** shut up in this*
           clauderēmur!   *prison!*

       ***utinam** adesset!*   ***If only** he **were** here!*
                                  Or, *I **wish** he **were** here!*

3   *with the present subjunctive (with or without **utinam**)*, indicating a wish about the FUTURE (negative **nē**):

       ***utinam** effugiant!*   ***May** they **escape**!*
                                  Or, ***If only** they **escape**!*

       vīvat rēx!   ***May** the king **live**!*
                                  Or, ***Long live** the king!*

14 Common Uses of the Cases

1   *nominative*:

    1a   indicating the *subject** of a verb:
       ***poēta** recitābat.*   ***The poet** was reciting.*

    1b   indicating a *complement* (see footnote to **18**.1b):
       Valerius est *senex*.   *Valerius is **an old man**.*

2   *vocative*, indicating a person or thing being spoken to:

       cavē, *domine*!   *Look out, **master**!*
       quid accidit, *Publī*?   *What happened, **Publius**?*

---

*The subject of an *active* verb is the person (thing, people) who does the action; the subject of a *passive* verb is the person (thing, people) to whom the action is done.

3 *genitive*

3a like "of" in English, indicating possession:
    gladiī *sociōrum meōrum*   *the swords **of my companions***

3b indicating the whole of something, of which a part or quantity has been mentioned:
    parum *cibī*   *too small a quantity **of food***
                             Or, in more natural English:
                             *too little **food***

3c in description, especially of non-physical qualities:
    eques *summae audāciae*   *a horseman **of the utmost boldness***
                             Or, in more natural English:
                             ***a very bold** horseman*

▌ *(Compare 6b.)*

3d with certain verbs** and adjectives[†]:
    patriae **oblīvīscar.**   *I shall forget **my country.***
    perītus *bellī*   *having experience **of war***
                             Or, *expert **in warfare***

3e indicating the value placed on something:
    honōrēs *parvī* **aestimō.**   *I consider honors **of little value.***
                             Or, in more natural English:
                             *I care **little** for honors.*

▌ *(Compare 6j.)*

Further examples:

1 castra hostium	3 immemor perīculī
2 vir sexāgintā annōrum	4 satis pecūniae

4 *dative*

4a like "to" in English, indicating the *indirect object* of a verb (i.e. a person or thing involved in the action, other than the subject or direct object):
    uxōrī **pecūniam reddidī.**   *I returned the money **to my wife.***

** e.g. **meminī** *I remember;* **misereor** *I pity;* **oblīvīscor** *I forget;* and the impersonal verbs listed in **19**.1c.

† e.g. **avidus** *covetous of;* **cupidus** *fond of;* **ignārus** *ignorant (of);* **memor** *mindful (of), remembering,* and **immemor** *forgetful (of);* **perītus** *skillful (in), experienced (in);* **plēnus** *full (of);* **similis** *like* and **dissimilis** *unlike* (**plēnus** can also be used with the ablative; **similis** and **dissimilis** can also be used with the dative.). See also **33**.1.

4b with certain verbs* and adjectives[†]:

lēgibus pārēmus.   *We are obedient **to the laws**.*
                          *Or, We obey **the laws**.*

populō cārus erat.   *He was dear **to the people**.*
                            *Or, He was loved **by the people**.*

4c in certain phrases with forms of the verb **sum** *I am*[§] (this is known as the *predicative* use of the dative):

faber _magnō auxiliō_ erit.   *The workman will be **a great help**.*
rēgēs omnibus _odiō_ erant.   *The kings were **hateful** to everybody.*
                                   *Or, Everybody **hated** the kings.*

dignitās tua mihi _cūrae_ est.   *Your dignity is **a matter of concern**
                                       to me.*

4d indicating the person for whose advantage or disadvantage something is done:

servus _nōbīs_ iānuam aperuit.   *The slave opened the door **for us**.*
fūrēs _mihi_ omnia abstulērunt.   *The thieves stole everything*
                                       __from me__.

4e with a nominative and forms of **est** *there is*, indicating possession:

est _tibi_ magna vīlla.   *There is a large villa **(belonging)**
                                to you.*
                               Or, in more natural English:
                               ***You** have a large villa.*

erat _nōbīs_ nūlla spēs.   *__We__ had no hope.*
sunt _mercātōrī_ multae gemmae.   ***The merchant** has many jewels.*
cōnsulēs, _quibus_ est summa   *the consuls, **who** have supreme*
** potestās**   *power*

---

*see examples listed in **34.3**.

†e.g. **cārus** *dear (to)*; **fidēlis** *faithful (to)*; **grātus** *pleasing (to), acceptable (to)*; **iūcundus** *delightful (to), pleasing (to)*; **similis** *similar (to), like* and **dissimilis** *dissimilar (to), unlike*; **ūtilis** *useful (to)* (**similis** and **dissimilis** can also be used with the genitive.). See also **33.2**.

§e.g.

auxiliō esse	*to be a help*
cūrae esse	*to be a cause for anxiety*
dolōrī esse	*to be a cause for grief*
exemplō esse	*to be an example*
exitiō esse	*to be a cause of ruin*
honōrī esse	*to be an honor*
impedimentō esse	*to be a hindrance*
odiō esse	*to be hateful*
salūtī esse	*to be a means of safety*
ūsuī esse	*to be useful*

See also **32**.

4f with the gerundive, indicating the person by whom something has to be done:

mīlitibus plaustrum reficiendum erat.	*For the soldiers, there was a wagon needing to be repaired.*

Or, in more natural English:

The soldiers had to repair a wagon.

▌ (For further examples, see **26**.2b.)

Further examples:

1 iuvenis patrī aurum trādidit.
2 captīvīs parcere nōlō.
3 ille centuriō mīlitibus odiō est.
4 est mihi nāvis ingēns.
5 ancilla hospitibus vīnum effundēbat.
6 medicō cōnfīdimus.
7 latrō mercātōrī dēnāriōs ēripuit.
8 templum nōbīs aedificandum est.

5   accusative

5a indicating the *object* (or *direct object*) of an active verb (i.e. the person or thing to whom the action is done):

amīcōs prōdidistī.	*You betrayed your friends.*

5b indicating how long something goes on:

multās hōrās iter faciēbam.	*I was traveling for many hours.*

▌ (Compare 6d; and for further examples, see **15**.1a.)

5c with certain prepositions:

per *aquam*	*through the water*
in *urbem*	*into the city*

▌ (Compare 6e; and for further examples, see **15**.2a and **16**.1 and 3.)

5d in indirect statements:

scio *hominem* **dormīre.**	*I know the man to be asleep.*

Or, in more natural English:

I know that the man is asleep.

▌ (For further examples, see **25**.4.)

5e in measurements:

mūrus *ducentōs pedēs* **altus**	*a wall 200 feet high*

5f in certain nouns and place-names, indicating a place to which there is movement:

rūs	*to the country*
Dēvam	*to Chester*

▌ (For further examples, see **15**.2d(i).)

6   *ablative*

6a   like "by" or "with" in English, indicating the method or instrument
by which something is done:*
clāmōribus **excitātus**	*awakened by the shouts*
hastīs **armātī**	*armed with spears*

6b   in description, especially of physical qualities:
homō *vultū sevērō*	*a man with a stern expression*

   (Compare 3c.)

6c   like English *from*, indicating the origin of someone or something:
clārā gente **nātus**	*born from a famous family*

6d   indicating the time at which (or within which) something happens:
tertiō mēnse **revēnit.**	*He returned in the third month.*

   (Compare 5b; and for further examples, see **15**.1b.)

6e   with certain prepositions:
ex *hortīs*	*out of the gardens*
in *Britanniā*	*in Britain*

   (Compare 5c; and for further examples, see **15**.2b and c and **16**.2 and 3.)

6f   in comparisons:
perītior *frātre* **sum.**	*I am more skillful than my brother.*

   (A commoner way of expressing the same idea is **perītior sum quam
   frāter.**)

6g   with certain verbs[†] and adjectives[§]:
dignus *suppliciō*	*worthy of punishment*
nāvibus **ūtēbantur.**	*They were using ships.*
cibō **carēmus.**	*We are without food.*

6h   in certain nouns and place-names, indicating a place from which
there is movement:
domō	*from home*
Pompēiīs	*from Pompeii*

   (For further examples, see **15**.2d(ii).)

---

* The preposition **ā, ab** is used with the ablative to indicate a *person* by whom
something is done:
ab *amīcīs* **excitātus**	*awakened by friends*
ā duce **armātī**	*armed by the leader*

   If the action is done by an *animal*, **ā, ab** may be either included or left out:
cane **excitātus** = *ā cane* **excitātus**	*awakened by the dog*

† e.g. **careō** *I am without, I lack;* and the deponent verbs **fruor** *I enjoy;* **fungor**
I carry out, I perform; **ūtor** *I use;* **vēscor** *I feed (on).* See also **34**.4.

§ e.g. **contentus** *satisfied (with);* **dignus** *worthy (of)* and **indignus** *unworthy (of);*
frētus *relying (on);* **plēnus** *full (of);* **vacuus** *free (from).* (**plēnus** can also be
used with the genitive.). See also **33**.3.

6j indicating the price at which something is bought or sold:

equum _vīlī pretiō_ ēmī.   *I bought the horse **at a cheap price**.*

(Compare 3e.)

6k indicating the extent by which two things differ from each other:

Marcus _multō_ stultior est   *Marcus is **much more** stupid than*
quam Sextus.   *Sextus.*

6m in *ablative absolute* phrases made up of (i) a noun or pronoun, and
(ii) an adjective, participle, or second noun, grammatically
disconnected from the rest of the sentence:

Caesare duce, mīlitēs urbem   ***With Caesar as leader**, the soldiers*
cēpērunt.   *captured the city.*
          Or, in more natural English:
          ***Under Caesar's leadership**, the*
          soldiers captured the city.

Pompēiō Crassōque   ***With Pompey and Crassus being***
cōnsulibus, rēs dīra   ***consuls**, a terrible thing happened.*
accidit.   Or, in more natural English:
          In the consulship of Pompey and
          ***Crassus**, a terrible thing happened.*

mē invītō, fīlius abiit.   ***With me unwilling**, my son went away.*
          Or, in more natural English:
          *My son went away **against my wishes**.*

nāve refectā, mercātor   ***With the ship having been repaired**,*
profectus est.   *the merchant set out.*
          Or, in more natural English:
          ***When the ship had been repaired**, the*
          merchant set out.

(For more examples of ablative absolute phrases containing participles,
see **20**.7.)

Further examples:

1 servus, vulnere impedītus, currere nōn poterat.
2 pictūram decem dēnāriīs vēndidī.
3 senex ingentī corpore prope iānuam stābat.
4 sextō diē nūntius ad vīllam vēnit.
5 haec puella multō callidior omnibus sorōribus est.
6 Boudicā rēgīnā, Britannī rebelliōnem contrā Rōmānōs fēcērunt.
7 tōtum templum flammīs cōnsūmptum est.
8 amīcus noster summā laude dignus erat.
9 tē duce, hostēs facile vincēmus!
10 Marcus, auxiliō amīcōrum ūsus, domum novam celeriter
aedificāvit.

7 For an exercise practicing the uses and forms of the different cases, see
1.7.

8 For examples of the use of the *locative* case, see **15**.2d(iii).

15 Time and Place

1 *time*

1a The *accusative* case (with or without **per**), indicates HOW LONG an action goes on:

duās hōrās **latēbam.**	*I lay hidden for two hours.*
quīnque diēs **nāvigābant.**	*They were sailing for five days.*

1b The *ablative* case indicates WHEN something happens:

sextā hōrā **profectī sunt.**	*They set off at the sixth hour.*
quārtō annō **bellī rēx mortuus est.**	*In the fourth year of the war, the king died.*

Further examples:

1 per tōtam noctem pugnāvimus.

2 quīntō diē amīcus advēnit.

3 octō annōs senex in urbe habitābat.

4 secundā hōrā ē lectō surrēxī.

1c The *ablative* case is also used to indicate the time WITHIN WHICH something happens:

tribus mēnsibus **revēnī.**	*I came back within three months.*

2 *place*

2a *in* or *ad with the accusative case** indicates the place TO which there is movement:

ad urbem	*to the city*	**in Graeciam**[†]	*to Greece*
ad Ītaliam	*to Italy*[†]	**ad forum**	*to the forum*

2b *ā, ab* or *ē, ex with the ablative case** indicates the place FROM which there is movement:

ex oppidō	*from/out of the town*	**ab Āfricā**	*from Africa*
ē Britanniā	*from/out of Britain*	**ā lītore**	*from the seashore*

2c *in with the ablative case** indicates the place WHERE something happens:

in Graeciā	*in Greece*	**in Galliā**	*in Gaul*
in templō	*in the temple*	**in viīs**	*in the streets*

---

* In verse, the prepositions **in, ad, ā, ab, ē, ex** are sometimes omitted:

terram Hesperiam **veniēs.**	*You will come to a land in the west.*
exarsit *dolor ossibus.*	*Grief flared up in his bones.*
proficīscitur *urbe.*	*He is setting out from the city.*

[†] **ad Ītaliam iit** means "he went (as far as but not in)to Italy"; **in Graeciam iit** means "he went (in)to Greece."

2d If the place-name is the name of a town or small island,* or is one of the nouns such as *domus, humus,* and *rūs,*

(i) the *accusative* case (without **ad** or **in**) indicates the place to which there is movement:

Dēvam	*to Chester*	**domum**	*home, homewards*
Pompēiōs	*to Pompeii*	**rūs**	*to the country*

(ii) the *ablative* case (without **ē, ex** or **ā, ab**) indicates the place from which there is movement:

Rōmā	*from Rome*	**domō**	*from home*
Athēnīs	*from Athens*	**rūre**	*from the country*

(iii) the *locative* case (whose formation is shown in **1**.10) indicates the place where something happens:

Alexandrīae	*in/at Alexandria*	**domī**	*at home*
Londiniī	*in London*	**rūrī**	*in the country*
Pompēiīs	*in/at Pompeii*	**humī**	*on the ground*

Further examples:

1 nēmō in forō erat; nam omnēs cīvēs ad amphitheātrum festīnābant.
2 mercātōrēs, ex Ītaliā profectī, in Siciliā duōs mēnsēs mānsērunt.
3 pater tuus heri rūre abiit, ut pompam Rōmae spectāret.
4 hodiē domī labōrō; crās tamen iter Athēnās faciam.
5 nūntiī prīmā lūce Pompēiīs discessērunt et Rōmam contendērunt.
6 centuriō, Dēvae in pugnā vulnerātus, in Galliam redīre temptāvit; Londiniī autem mortuus est.

---

*i.e. an island small enough to be regarded as a single place or containing no more than one town.

16 Common Prepositions

1 *used with the accusative case*

ad	*to, towards*
ante	*before*
apud	*at the house of; among*
circum	*around*
contrā	*against*
extrā	*outside*
inter	*among, between*
intrā	*inside*
per	*through*
post	*after, behind*
praeter	*past; except*
prope	*near*
propter	*on account of, because of*
trāns	*across*
ultrā	*beyond*

2 *used with the ablative case*

ā, ab	*from; by*
cum	*with*
dē	*down from; about*
ē, ex	*out of*
prō	*in front of; on behalf of*
sine	*without*

3 *used sometimes with the accusative, sometimes with the ablative*

in	(with accusative) *into;* (with ablative) *in*
super	*over*
sub	*under*

These prepositions are used with the accusative if movement is involved; otherwise with the ablative.

in forō **ambulābat.**	*She was walking **in the forum**.*
in forum **ruit.**	*She rushed **into the forum**.*
super mēnsam **saluit.**	*He jumped **over the table**.*
sub mēnsā **iacēbat.**	*He was lying **under the table**.*

17 Agreement

1 *agreement (in number) between nominative noun and verb*
servus *slave*   **servus** *labōrat.*   *The slave* **works.**
servus is singular; so the verb **labōrat** is also singular.

servī *slaves*   **servī** *labōrant.*   *The slaves* **work.**
servī is plural; so the verb **labōrant** is also plural.

2 *agreement (in case, gender and number) between noun and adjective*
captīvus *puellae* **crēdidit.**   *The prisoner trusted* **the girl.**
captīvus *puellae benignae* **crēdidit.**   *The prisoner trusted* **the kindly girl.**
puellae is dative, feminine and singular; so **benignae**, which describes
puellae, is also dative, feminine and singular.

mīlitēs **vīdī.**   *I saw* **the soldiers.**
mīlitēs ignāvōs **vīdī.**   *I saw* **the lazy soldiers.**
mīlitēs is accusative, masculine and plural; so **ignāvōs**, which
describes **mīlitēs**, is also accusative, masculine and plural.

▮   For an exercise practicing agreement between noun and adjective, see **2.6.**

3 *agreement (in case) between one noun (or noun + adjective phrase) and another*
Marcus **surrēxit.**   *Marcus stood up.*
Marcus centuriō **surrēxit.**   *Marcus the centurion stood up.*
Marcus is nominative; so the noun **centuriō**, which describes **Marcus**,
is also nominative. (This is sometimes described as *apposition*; **centuriō**
is said to be "in apposition" to **Marcus.**)

fūr *Sextum* **fallere nōn potuit.**   *The thief could not fool* **Sextus.**
fūr *Sextum, virum callidum,*   *The thief could not fool* **Sextus,**
   fallere nōn potuit.   *a cunning man.*
Sextum is accusative; so the phrase **virum callidum**, which is in
apposition to **Sextum**, is also accusative.

4 *agreement (in gender and number) between noun (or pronoun) and relative*
pronoun (whose forms are shown in **5.8**)
ancillae . . . **cantābant.**   *The* **slave-girls** *were singing.*
ancillae, *quae in culīnā*   *The slave-girls,* **who** *were working*
   labōrābant, cantābant.   *in the kitchen, were singing.*
ancillae is feminine plural; so **quae**, which refers to **ancillae**, is also
feminine plural (**ancillae** is described as the *antecedent* of **quae**).

puer . . . **rīsit.**   *The* **boy** *smiled.*
puer *cui* **discum dedī rīsit.**   *The boy* **to whom** *I gave a discus smiled.*
puer is masculine singular; so **cui**, which refers to **puer**, is also
masculine singular (**puer** is the antecedent of **cui**).

The *gender* and *number* of a relative pronoun are fixed by its antecedent,
as described above. But the *case* of a relative pronoun is fixed by the
way it fits into the relative clause. For instance, in the first example
above, **quae** is the subject of **labōrābant**, and is therefore nominative; in
the second example, **cui** is the indirect object of **dedī**, and is therefore
dative.

Further examples:

1 puella, quae in cubiculō dormiēbat, nihil audīvit.
2 hic est gladius quō rēx occīsus est.
3 gemmae, quās mercātor in Āfricā ēmerat, pretiōsissimae erant.
4 templum, quod in mediō oppidō stābat, saepe vīsitābam.
5 ubi sunt clientēs quibus heri cibum dedimus?
6 senex cuius pecūniam puerī invēnerant grātiās maximās eīs ēgit.

In each example, pick out the antecedent, and explain the gender, number, and case of the relative pronoun.

18 Attributive and Predicative Uses of Adjectives and Nouns

attributive	*predicative*
1a **magnus leō dormiēbat.** *The large lion was asleep.*	1b **leō est magnus.*** *The lion is large.*
2a **Sextus victor rīsit.** *The victorious Sextus smiled.*	2b **Sextus victor rediit.** *Sextus came back victorious.*
3a **mīles mortuus sepeliēbātur.** *The dead soldier was being buried.*	3b **mīles mortuus prōcubuit.** *The soldier fell down dead.*
4a **Publium cōnsulem cōnspexī.** *I spotted the consul Publius.*	4b **Publium cōnsulem creāvī.** *I appointed Publius (as) consul.*
5a **āthlētam fortissimum spectābant.** *They were watching a very brave athlete.*	5b **āthlētam fortissimum putābant.** *They thought the athlete very brave.*

6   To decide whether an adjective (or noun) is being used attributively or predicatively, it is necessary to look at *the whole sentence*. For instance: In sentence 3a an attributive translation (*The dead soldier was being buried.*) would normally make better sense than a predicative one (*The soldier was being buried dead.*) unless the circumstances were rather peculiar, e.g. if the speaker were denying an accusation that the soldier was being buried alive.
    Similarly, in sentence 4b a predicative translation (*I appointed Publius (as) consul.*) would normally make better sense than an attributive one (*I appointed the consul Publius.*).

7 Further examples:

1 in mediā pompā ambulābant septem captīvī. captīvus prīmus superbē circumspectābat; cēterī lacrimābant.
2 frāter tuus prīmus advēnit, ultimus discessit.
3 ubi Claudius appāruit, mīlitēs eum imperātōrem salūtāvērunt.
4 Claudius imperātor venēnō necātus est.

---

*A noun or adjective used predicatively with a form of **sum** *I am* or of such verbs as **fīō** *I become* or **videor** *I seem* is sometimes described as a *complement*, because it *completes* the sense of the sentence. For example, **magnus** is the complement in sentence 1b.

19 Impersonal Use of Verbs

1 *3rd person singular active forms*

1a *without a noun or pronoun*

advesperāscit.	*It is getting late.*
semper pluēbat.	*It was always raining.*
tonuit.	*It thundered.*

1b *with a noun or pronoun in the accusative case*
decet tē **deōs immortālēs honōrāre.**
*It is **proper that you** honor the immortal gods.*
Or, in more natural English:
***You ought** to honor the immortal gods.*

Rōmānōs **numquam** *oportet* **hostibus crēdere.**
*It is never **right that Romans** trust the enemy.*
Or, ***Romans must** never trust the enemy.*

1c *with a noun or pronoun in the accusative case* (indicating the person who feels an emotion *and another in the genitive* (indicating the cause of the emotion):
coquum **stultitiae** *pudēbat.*
***It made the cook ashamed** of his stupidity.*
Or, ***The cook was ashamed** of his stupidity.*

puellam **cibī vīnīque** *taedet.*
***It makes the girl tired** of food and wine.*
Or, ***The girl is tired** of food and wine.*

The five verbs used in this way are:

miseret (mē)	*it makes me feel pity,* or *I pity, I am sorry for*
paenitet (mē)	*it makes me regret,* or *I regret, I am sorry about*
piget (mē)	*it vexes me,* or *I am vexed at*
pudet (mē)	*it makes me ashamed,* or *I am ashamed of*
taedet (mē)	*it makes me tired,* or *I am tired of*

See **34**.1c.

1d *with a noun or pronoun in the dative case*
libet mihi **hoc dōnum accipere.**
***It is agreeable** to me to receive this present.*
Or, *I **am glad** to receive this present.*

placuit nōbīs **fugere.**
***It pleased us** to run away,* or ***We decided** to run away.*

iuvenibus **iam** *licet* **redīre.**
*It is now **permitted to the young men** to come back.*
Or, ***The young men may** now come back.*
See **34**.1d and 1e.

Further examples:

1 cotīdiē pluit.
2 semper oportet nōs fidem servāre.
3 patrī meō libet prope mare habitāre.
4 nōlīte intrāre! decet vōs extrā iānuam manēre.
5 rēgem crūdēlitātis nōn pudēbat.
6 nōn licuit mihi vīnum bibere.
7 mīlitibus placuit ā castrīs discēdere.
8 fūrem sceleris iam paenitet.

2 *3rd person singular passive forms,* used to indicate an action without
indicating the doer of the action:

curritur. *It is being run.*
Or, in more natural English:
Running is taking place, a race is going on, etc.

pugnātum est. *It was fought.*
Or, in more natural English:
Fighting took place, a battle was fought, etc.

tibi parcētur. *Mercy will be shown to you.*
Or, in more natural English:
You will be shown mercy, you will be spared.

20 Uses of the Participles

1 *present participle*

canis dominum *intrantem* vīdit.
*The dog saw his master **entering**.*

prīncipī ē Campāniā *redeuntī* complūrēs senātōrēs obviam iērunt.
*Several senators went to meet the emperor **returning** from Campania.*
Or, ***When** the emperor **was returning** from Campania, several senators went to
meet him.*

2   *perfect active participle*

> **senex, multās iniūriās *passus,* auxilium ā patrōnō petīvit.**
> *The old man, **having suffered** many acts of injustice, sought help from his patron.*

3   *perfect passive participle*

> **fūrēs, ad iūdicem *ductī,* veniam petīvērunt.**
> *The thieves, **having been led** to the judge, begged for mercy.*

> **ānulum *inventum* ad centuriōnem attulimus.**
> *We brought the ring, **having been found,** to the centurion.*
> Or, in more natural English:
> *When the ring **had been found,** we brought it to the centurion.*

4   *future participle*

> **mercātōrēs nāvem *cōnscēnsūrōs* vīdī.**
> *I saw the merchants **about to go on board** the ship.*

5   Each of the participles in paragraphs 1–4 refers to a noun. For instance, in the first example in paragraph 1, **intrantem** refers to **dominum**. A participle agrees in case, gender, and number with the noun it refers to; in paragraph 1 **dominum** is accusative masculine singular, and so **intrantem** is also accusative masculine singular.

6   Sometimes the noun or pronoun to which the participle refers is not mentioned in the sentence:

> **ingēns multitūdō *fugientium* viās omnēs complēvit.**
> *A huge crowd **of (people) running away** filled all the streets.*

> **ab amīcīs *incitātus,* in Circō Maximō certāvit.**
> ***Having been urged on** by his friends, he competed in the Circus Maximus.*

7   *participle used with noun or pronoun in ablative absolute phrase,* grammatically disconnected from the rest of the sentence:

> **ānulō inventō, omnēs gaudēbant.**
> ***With the ring having been found,** everyone was glad.*
> Or, in more natural English:
> ***When the ring had been found,** everyone was glad.*

> (If **ānulō inventō** were omitted from this example, the remaining words **omnēs gaudēbant** would still make a complete sentence. Compare the second example in paragraph 3, which would no longer make a complete sentence if **ānulum inventum** were omitted.)

> **duce loquente, nūntius accurrit.**
> ***With the leader speaking,** a messenger came dashing up.*
> Or, ***While the leader was speaking,** a messenger came dashing up.*

dominā ēgressā, **servī garrīre coepērunt.**
With the mistress having gone out, the slaves began to chatter.
Or, *After the mistress had gone out, the slaves began to chatter.*

mīlitibus īnstrūctīs, **tuba sonuit.**
With the soldiers having been drawn up, a trumpet sounded.
Or, *When the soldiers had been drawn up, a trumpet sounded.*

> For examples of ablative absolute phrases containing adjectives and pairs of nouns, see **14.6m.**

8   *examples of different ways of translating participles*

forum ingressī, ...   Having entered the forum, ...
                                When they had entered the forum, ...
                                After entering the forum, ...
                                They entered the forum and . . . .
                                Because they had entered the forum, ...
                                Although they had entered the forum, ...
                                On entering the forum, ...
                                On their entry into the forum, they . . . .   *etc.*

in hortō labōrāns, ...   Working in the garden, ...
                                While working in the garden, ...
                                As he was working in the garden, ...
                                During his work in the garden, he . . . .   *etc.*

The most suitable way of translating a participle in any sentence depends on the sense of the sentence as a whole.

9   Further examples:

1 statuae deōrum, ex aurō factae, ad templum portābantur.
2 ponte dēlētō, nēmō flūmen trānsīre poterat.
3 ecce! duōs elephantōs videō per viam prōcēdentēs.
4 dux, mīlitēs hortātus, prīncipia intrāvit.
5 poētā recitante, fūr pecūniam spectātōribus auferēbat.
6 puer, pugnantium clāmōre perterritus, fūgit.
7 Rōmānī urbem captam incendērunt.
8 Rōmānī, urbe captā, valdē gaudēbant.
9 senex moritūrus fīliōs ad sē vocāvit.
10 iuvenem, hastā vulnerātum, ad medicum dūximus.
11 amīcō ex Italiā discēdentī centum dēnāriōs dedī.
12 ab Imperātōre ipsō laudāta, rīsit.

Pick out the participle in each sentence, and identify the noun (if any) that it describes. Which sentences contain ablative absolute phrases?

10   > For examples of different types of word order in sentences containing participles, see **28.2 and 3.**

21 Uses of the Infinitives*

1 *with verbs such as **possum** "I am able," **volō** "I want," **dēbeō** "I must," **timeō** "I am afraid," etc.:*

crās *proficīscī* volō.	I want **to set off** tomorrow.
senex *festīnāre* nōn poterat.	The old man was unable **to hurry**.
Or,	The old man could not **hurry**.
iuvenis *respondēre* timēbat.[†]	The young man was afraid **to reply**.

2 *with **nōlī**, **nōlīte**, ordering somebody not to do something (as described in **12**.2):*

nōlī mē *culpāre!*	Don't **put the blame on** me!
nōlīte hīc *manēre!*	Don't **stay** here!

3 *with phrases such as **decōrum est**, **difficile est**, etc.:*

difficile mihi erit aequō animō *loquī.*	It will be difficult for me **to speak** calmly.

4 *with impersonal verbs such as **placet**, **licet**, etc. (**19**.1):*

līberīs *exīre* nōn licuit.	The children were not allowed **to go out**.

5 *with **iubeō** "I order" and **vetō** "I forbid, I order. . . not" (**25**.3):*

rēx nōs *comprehendī* iussit.	The king ordered us **to be arrested**.
mercātor nautās vīnum *bibere* vetuit.	The merchant told the sailors not **to drink** the wine.

6 *as a "historical" infinitive*, indicating one or more actions in the past, usually in vivid or quickly-moving narrative:

tum dēmum omnēs *dēspērāre; in viās ruere, clāmāre*, hūc illūc *currere*.
*Then at last **they were all in despair; they were rushing** into the streets, **shouting** and **running** this way and that.*

---

*For further examples of some of these uses, see the paragraph referred to under each sub-heading.

†For examples of another way of using verbs meaning "I am afraid," see **23**.8.

7   *to express indirect statements* (**25**.4):

hospitēs ancillam optimē *cantāvisse* **putāvērunt.**
*The guests thought that the slave-girl **had sung** excellently.*

crēdō mīlitēs fidem *servātūrōs esse.*
*I believe that the soldiers **will keep** their word.*

8   Further examples:

1   facile erat sacerdōtibus vērum cognōscere.
2   nōn licet vōbīs in viā lūdere.
3   nōlī mē tangere!
4   nāvem reficere tandem poterāmus.
5   centuriō audīvit omnēs captīvōs effūgisse.
6   pecūniam patrī reddere dēbēs.
7   dux epistulam statim scrībī iussit.
8   spectātōrēs īrātissimī erant. exclāmāre; gladiātōrem vituperāre; etiam lapidēs iacere; tōtum amphitheātrum strepitū complērī.

22 Main Clauses and Subordinate Clauses

1   *sentences consisting of a main clause only*

cīvēs conveniēbant.	*The citizens were gathering.*
senex medicum arcessīvit.	*The old man sent for the doctor.*

2   *sentences consisting of a main clause and subordinate clause*

coquus numquam labōrat, *quod semper dormit.*
*The cook never works, **because he is always asleep.***

haruspicēs, *cum victimam īnspexissent*, ōmina nūntiāvērunt.
*The soothsayers, **when they had inspected the victim**, announced the omens.*

Or, ***After inspecting the victim***, *the soothsayers announced the omens.*

Each of these sentences is made up of:

(i) a *main clause*, i.e. a group of words which would make a complete sentence on its own (**coquus numquam labōrat** in the first example, and **haruspicēs ōmina nūntiāvērunt** in the second);

(ii) a *subordinate clause*, i.e. a group of words introduced by a word like **quod** or **cum** (*quod semper dormit* in the first example, and *cum victimam īnspexissent* in the second). A subordinate clause on its own cannot make a complete sentence.

Further examples:

1   mercātor amīcōs ad cēnam invītāvit quod diem nātālem celebrābat.
2   iuvenis, simulac nōmen suum audīvit, surrēxit.
3   quamquam servī multum frūmentum in horreum intulerant, dominus nōn erat contentus.
4   tot vīllās habeō ut eās nūmerāre nōn possim.

In each sentence, pick out the main clause and subordinate clause.

3   A Latin sentence may contain more than one subordinate clause:

quamquam appropinquābant hostēs, quī hastās vibrābant, **centuriō immōtus manēbat.**
*The centurion remained motionless, **although the enemy were approaching, who were brandishing spears**.*

centuriō immōtus manēbat is the main clause; the other two groups of words are subordinate clauses.

4   For examples of different types of word order in sentences containing main clauses and subordinate clauses, see **28.1–4.**

23 Common Types of Subordinate Clause

1 *relative clauses*, usually introduced by forms of the relative pronoun **quī**
(shown in **5**.8) or relative adverbs such as **ubi**:

mīlitēs *quōs imperātor mīserat* in castrīs manēbant.
*The soldiers **whom the emperor had sent** remained in the camp.*

prope iānuam stābat nūntius, *cui epistulam trādidī*.
*Near the door stood a messenger, **to whom I handed the letter**.*

haec est domus *ubi lībertus meus habitat*.
*This is the house **where my freedman lives**.*

> For examples of agreement between antecedent and relative pronoun,
> see **17**.4.

Forms of **is** are often used as antecedents to forms of **quī**:

***is quī* illam fābulam nārrāvit mentiēbātur.**
***He who** told that story was lying.*
Or, ***The man who** told that story was lying.*

***eī quī* fūgērunt mox capientur.**
***Those who** ran away will soon be caught.*

***id quod* nauta dīxit nōs maximē perturbāvit.**
***That which** the sailor said alarmed us very much.*
Or, ***What** the sailor said alarmed us very much.*

***eās* vīllās vēndidī *quae* mē minimē dēlectābant.**
*I sold **those** villas **that** least appealed to me.*

> For examples of sentences in which the antecedent comes after the
> relative clause or is omitted altogether, see **28**.1c.

Similar to the use of **is** with **quī** is the use of **tantus** with **quantus, tam**
with **quam, tot** with **quot**, etc.:

fīlius meus *tam* fortis est *quam* leō.
*My son is **as** brave **as** a lion.*

***tot* agricolae aderant *quot* mīlitēs.**
*There were **as** many farmers present **as** soldiers.*

***tantum* praemium tū accēpistī *quantum* ego.**
*You received **as** big a reward **as** I did.*

Further examples:

1 ubi est liber quem heri legēbam?
2 puella quae adstābat senem salūtāvit.
3 captīvī quōs rēx ē carcere līberāverat maximās grātiās eī ēgērunt.
4 omnēs cīvēs imperātōrī, quī urbī iam appropinquābat, obviam iērunt.
5 id quod dīcis falsum est.
6 nihil est tam perīculōsum quam mare.

> For examples of a different way of using the relative pronoun (the
> *connecting* use), see **5**.8.
>
> For examples of forms of **quī** used with the subjunctive in purpose
> clauses and result clauses, see paragraphs 2 and 3 below.

2 *purpose clauses* (sometimes called *final* clauses), introduced by **ut**, **nē**, or forms of **quī** or other relative words, followed by a subjunctive form of the verb in the present or imperfect tense:

imperātor ipse adest *ut fābulam spectet.*
*The emperor himself is here **in order that he may watch the play.***
Or, *The emperor himself is here **to watch the play.***

mīlitēs ēmīsit *quī turbam dēpellerent.*
*He sent out soldiers **who were to drive the crowd away.***
Or, *He sent out soldiers **to drive the crowd away.***

fēlēs arborem ascendit *nē ā puerīs caperētur.*
*The cat climbed up a tree **so that it should not be caught by the boys.***
Or, *The cat climbed up a tree **in order not to be caught by the boys.***

Further examples:

1 fabrī tōtam noctem labōrāvērunt ut templum ante lūcem perficerent.
2 coquus aquam attulit quā flammae exstinguerentur.
3 dēsilite in hanc fossam, ut hastās hostium vītētis!
4 domum tacitī intrāvimus, nē ā cane audīrēmur.

> Purpose clauses containing the comparative form of an adjective or adverb are normally introduced by **quō**:
> **nāvem condūxī**, *quō celerius ad Ītaliam revenīrem.*
> *I hired a ship, **in order to return to Italy more quickly**.*

3 *result clauses* (sometimes called *consecutive* clauses), expressed by **ut*** and a subjunctive form of the verb, usually in the present or imperfect tense:

tam perītus est faber *ut ab omnibus laudētur.*
*The craftsman is so skillful **that he is praised by everybody.***

tanta erat nūbēs *ut pāstōrēs sōlem vidēre nōn possent.*
*The cloud was so great **that the shepherds could not see the sun.***

When a main clause contains one of the following words, it often leads on to a result clause:

tam	*so*	**tot**	*so many*
tālis	*such*	**adeō**	*so* (= to such an extent)
tantus	*so big, so great*	**ita, sīc**	*so* (= in such a way)

---

*Some types of result clause are introduced by forms of **quī** (meaning "of the sort who . . .," etc.):

nōn is est *quī terreātur.*   *He is not a person **of the sort who is scared.***
     Or, *He is not **such a man as to be scared.***

erant *quī resisterent.*   *There were people **of such a sort as to resist.***
     Or, more naturally, ***Some people resisted.***

Further examples:

1 tantus erat clāmor ut nēmō verba rēgis audīret.
2 gladiātor spectātōrēs adeō dēlectāvit ut iterum iterumque plauderent.
3 tam benignus es ut ab omnibus cīvibus amēris.
4 tot vulnera accēperam ut medicus dē vītā meā dēspērāret.

4 *causal clauses*, indicating a cause or reason, expressed by **quod** or **quia** *because* and an indicative form of the verb, or by **cum** *since* and a subjunctive:

imperātor Agricolae invidēbat *quod multās rēs splendidās gesserat.*
*The emperor was jealous of Agricola **because he had done many splendid deeds.***

asinus, *quia obstinātus erat,* **prōgredī nōluit.**
*The donkey, **because it was obstinate**, refused to go on.*

tibi, *cum amīcus sīs,* **pecūniam meam mandābō.**
*I shall entrust my money to you, **since you are my friend**.*

quod and **quia** are also used with the *subjunctive* to quote a reason put forward by some other person or people, with whom the speaker may or may not happen to agree:

Socratēs damnātus est *quod* **iuvenēs** *corrumperet.*
*Socrates was condemned **because** (according to his accusers) **he corrupted** young men.*

(Compare this with a causal clause in which the *indicative* is used:

Socratēs damnātus est *quod* **iuvenēs** *corrumpēbat.*
*Socrates was condemned **because** (in fact) **he corrupted** young men.*)

Further examples:

1 candidātō vestrō nōn faveō, quia mendāx est.
2 māter fīlium vituperāvit quod tardus ē lectō surrēxisset.
3 māter fīlium vituperāvit quod tardus ē lectō surrēxerat.

5   *temporal clauses,* indicating the time at which something happens,
    introduced by such words as:

ubi *when* (followed by an indicative form of the verb)
postquam *after*   „
simulac, simulatque *as soon as*   „
antequam, priusquam *before*   „
dōnec *until*   „
dum *until, while*   „
cum *when* (followed by a subjunctive in the imperfect or pluperfect
tense)

simulac rēx ātrium intrāvit, **omnēs surrēxērunt.**
As soon as the king came into the hall, everybody stood up.

in tabernā vīnum bibēbam *dōnec uxor caupōnis mē ēiēcit.*
*I was drinking wine in the inn **until the innkeeper's wife threw me out.***

mercātōrēs, *cum cōnsilium audīvissent,* **libenter cōnsēnsērunt.**
***When the merchants had heard the plan,** they willingly agreed.*

> **antequam** and **priusquam** are sometimes split into separate words,
> **ante . . . quam** and **prius . . . quam:**
>   **nūntiī ante discessērunt** *quam sōl ortus est.*
>   *The messengers left **before the sun rose.***
>
> A Latin perfect tense after **postquam, simulac,** or **ubi** is often translated
> by an English pluperfect:
>   **dominus,** *postquam fundum īnspexit,* **ad urbem rediit.**
>   *After the master had inspected the farm, he went back to the city.*

priusquam, dum, and **dōnec** are used with the subjunctive to add the
idea of purpose to the idea of time:

exspectābant *dum sacerdōs signum daret.*
*They were waiting **until the priest should give the signal.***
Or, *They were waiting **for the priest to give the signal.***

fugiendum est nōbīs *priusquam custōdēs nōs cōnspiciant.*
*We must run away **before the guards catch sight of us.***

dum meaning "while" (i.e. "at one point during the time that . . .") is
used with a present tense even if the sentence refers to past time:

dum bellum in Britanniā geritur, **rēs dīra Rōmae accidit.**
***While the war was being waged in Britain,** a terrible disaster
happened at Rome.*

Further examples:

1 hospitēs, ubi cibum gustāvērunt, coquum valdē laudāvērunt.
2 centuriō, cum fenestram frāctam cōnspexisset, vehementer saeviēbat.
3 cīvēs, simulatque ad apodytērium revēnērunt, vestīmenta induērunt.
4 rēx, postquam epistulam servō dictāvit, nūntium arcessīvit.
5 fūr, priusquam caperētur, ē vīllā ruit.
6 dum pāstor dormit, lupī duōs agnōs rapuērunt.

> **cum** *when* is used with an *indicative* form of the verb to introduce the following four types of temporal clause:
>
> (i) *referring to present or future time*
>
> **cum sorōrem tuam vīderō, epistulam eī referam.**
> **When I see your sister, I shall deliver the letter to her.**
>
> (ii) *placed after the main clause and indicating the chief event of the sentence*
>
> **paene domum pervēnerat, cum subitō latrōnēs ex īnsidiīs ērūpērunt.**
> **He had almost reached home, when suddenly robbers burst out from an ambush.**
>
> (iii) *strongly emphasizing the idea of time*
>
> **cum tū in lectō dormiēbās, eō tempore nōs in agrīs labōrābāmus.**
> **At the time when you were asleep in bed, we were toiling in the fields.**
>
> (iv) *meaning "whenever . . . ,"* followed by a verb in the PLUPERFECT tense if the verb in the main clause is *past*, and by a verb in the PERFECT tense if the main verb is *present*:
>
> **cum puer errāverat, magister eum pūniēbat.**
> **Whenever the boy made a mistake, the teacher used to punish him.**
>
> **cum eum salūtāvī, mē vituperat.**
> **Whenever I greet him, he is rude to me.**

6   *concessive clauses* (indicating "although . . ."), expressed by **quamquam** and an indicative form, or by **quamvīs** or **cum** with a subjunctive:

canis, *quamquam ferōciter restitit*, ā lupō superātus est.
Although the dog resisted fiercely, it was overcome by the wolf.

cum *in rīpā flūminis habitāret*, tamen nāvigāre nesciēbat.
Although he lived on the bank of a river, he still didn't know how to sail.

Further examples:

1   quamquam marītus tuus in carcere adhūc retinētur, nōlī dēspērāre!
2   quamvīs morbō afflīgerētur, senex ad forum ambulāre cōnātus est.
3   mīlitēs, quamquam itinere fessī erant, ad pugnandum sē īnstrūxērunt.

> Sentences containing concessive clauses introduced by **etsī** *even if, even though* are expressed in the same ways as conditional sentences (described in **24**):
>
> **etsī *mihi mīlle dēnāriōs obtulissēs*, ānulum numquam tibi vēndidissem.**
> *Even if you had offered me a thousand denarii, I would never have sold you the ring.*
>
> **etsī *magna turba puellae obstābat*, ad portum mox pervēnit.**
> *Even though a large crowd obstructed the girl, she soon reached the port.*

7   *comparative clauses*, expressed by **sīcut** *just as* or **ut** *as* (often accompanied by **ita** *so*) and an indicative form, to make a comparison with an actual event, or by **quasi, tamquam** *as if, as though* and a subjunctive form, to make a comparison with an imaginary event:

servī in agrīs labōrābant, *sīcut dominus iusserat*.
*The slaves were working in the fields, **just as the master had ordered**.*

ut *fēlēs mūrem petit*, ita gladiātor adversārium agitāvit.
As a cat chases a mouse, so did the gladiator pursue his opponent.

centuriō mē salūtāvit *quasi amīcissimus essem*.
*The centurion greeted me **as if I were his dearest friend**.*

Further examples:

1   ut pater mē docuit, ita ego tē docēbō.
2   puerī fūgērunt quasi umbram vīdissent.
3   ut avēs per caelum volant, ita nāvēs per undās ruēbant.
4   amīcus meus erat victor, sīcut spērāveram.

> For examples of comparison expressed by **tantus . . . quantus, tot . . . quot**, etc., see paragraph 1 above.

75

8 *clauses of fear and danger*, introduced by **nē*** followed by a subjunctive form to express a fear that something MAY happen, IS happening, or HAS happened:

> **avārus verēbātur** *nē fūr aurum invenīret.*
> *The miser was afraid lest a thief would find his gold.*[†]

Or, in more natural English:
> *The miser was afraid that a thief would find his gold.*

> **perīculum est** *nē barbarī oppidum capiant.*
> *There is a danger that the barbarians may capture the town.*[†]

> **puellae timent** *nē amīca in morbum gravem inciderit.*
> *The girls fear that their friend has fallen seriously ill.*

nē nōn* (sometimes **ut**) is used to express fear that something may NOT happen, is NOT happening, or has NOT happened:

> **timēbāmus** $\begin{cases} \textit{nē pater nōn superfuisset.} \\ \textit{ut pater superfuisset.} \end{cases}$
> *We were afraid that our father had not survived.*

Further examples:

1 perīculum erat nē nāvēs tempestāte dēlērentur.
2 mercātor timēbat nē iuvenis pecūniam nōn redderet.
3 timeō nē nūntius ab hostibus captus sit.
4 verēbāmur nē parentēs nostrī in flammīs periissent.

> For an example of another way of using verbs meaning "I am afraid," see **21.1**.

---

* The reason why **nē** is used for a POSITIVE fear, and **nē nōn** (or **ut**) for a NEGATIVE fear, is that clauses of fear are used to express a wish, and the speaker wishes the *opposite* of what he fears. For example, "I fear that he may find me" implies "May he *not* find me!" and the Latin is **timeō** *nē mē inveniat.*

†These sentences could also mean ". . . was afraid that a thief *was* finding his gold" and ". . . danger that the barbarians *are* capturing the town." The surrounding context normally makes the speaker's meaning clear.

9 Further examples of the types of subordinate clause described in paragraphs 1–8:

1 servī in viam contendērunt ut pompam spectārent.
2 sacerdōs, postquam victimam sacrificāvit, deōs precātus est.
3 quamquam ancilla suāviter cantābat, hospitēs nōn dēlectābantur.
4 tam obscūra est nox ut nihil vidēre possim.
5 medicus, cum dentēs meōs extrāxisset, duōs dēnāriōs postulāvit.
6 faber diū tacēbat, quasi rem difficillimam cōgitāret.
7 spectātōrēs āthlētam vituperābant quod fraude vīcerat.
8 spectātōrēs āthlētam vituperābant quod fraude vīcisset.
9 fugite, nē ab inimīcīs interficiāminī!
10 agricola, cum ad vīllam regrederētur, lupum ingentem cōnspexit.
11 homō cuius domus ardēbat auxilium ā praetereuntibus petīvit.
12 rēgīna, quamvīs īrāta esset, mihi tandem ignōvit.
13 fēmina magistrum ēlēgit quī fīliōs docēret.
14 timēbāmus nē ab hostibus circumvenīrēmur.
15 eī quī mentīrī solent, saepe ipsī dēcipiuntur.
16 iuvenēs frūstrā exspectābant dōnec amīcus redīret.

What type of subordinate clause is being used in each example?

10 For examples of subordinate clauses used to express indirect question and indirect command, see **25**.2 and 3.

11 For examples of subordinate clauses used inside indirect speech, see **25**.7.

12 For examples of conditional clauses, see **24**.1–2.

24 Conditional Sentences

Normally made up of (i) a main clause, and (ii) a conditional clause introduced by **sī** *if* or **nisi** *unless, if . . . not:*

1 *with indicative forms of the verb*

1a *in a past tense*
sī amīcus tuus testāmentum *finxit,* **scelus grave** *commīsit.*
If your friend **forged** *the will,* **he has committed** *a serious crime.*

1b *in the present tense*
sī *valēs, gaudeō.*
If **you are well, I am pleased.**

1c *in the future or future perfect tense* (often translated, in a conditional clause, by an English present tense)
sī illud iterum *fēceris,* **tē** *pūniam.*
If **you do** *that again,* **I shall punish** *you.*

sī in urbe *manēbit,* **in perīculō** *erit.*
If **he stays** *in the city,* **he will be** *in danger.*

nisi imperātor novās cōpiās *mīserit, opprimēmur.*
If the emperor **does** *not* **send** *reinforcements,* **we shall be overwhelmed.**
Or, *Unless the emperor* **sends** *reinforcements,* **we shall be overwhelmed.**

Further examples:

1 sī ancilla dormit, excitā eam!
2 sī dē equō tuō dēcideris, cēterī puerī tē dērīdēbunt.
3 sī frātrēs meī in Britanniā mīlitābunt, miserrimī erunt.
4 nisi nāvēs ad portum mox pervēnerint, tempestāte dēlēbuntur.

1d *in two different tenses* (main clause referring to one time, and conditional clause to another):
sī aeger *es,* **medicum** *arcessam.*
If **you are** *ill,* **I will send for** *a doctor.*

2 *with subjunctive forms of the verb* (normally translated in the main clause by an English form involving "would" or "should")

2a *in the pluperfect tense of the subjunctive,* referring to PAST time:
sī in eōdem locō *mānsissēs*, perīculum *vītāvissēs*.
*If **you had stayed** in the same place, **you would have avoided** the danger.*

sī dīligentius *labōrāvissem*, dominus mē *līberāvisset*.
*If **I had worked** harder, my master **would have freed** me.*

magister, nisi nimis vīnī *bibisset*, in flūmen nōn *cecidisset*.
*If the teacher **had** not **drunk** too much wine, **he would** not **have fallen** into the river.*

Further examples:

1 sī equōs vēndidissēs, multam pecūniam accēpissēs.
2 nisi coquus circumspectāvisset, cibus ā cane raptus esset.
3 sī nūntiī māne profectī essent, Londinium ante noctem pervēnissent.
4 sī Caesar nōbīs praefuisset, hostēs superāvissēmus.

2b *in the imperfect tense of the subjunctive,* referring to PRESENT time:
sī Rōmae nunc *habitārem*, clientēs mē assiduē *vexārent*.
*If **I were living** in Rome now, my clients **would be** continually **pestering** me.*

sī Domitiānus nōs adhūc *regeret*, miserrimī *essēmus*.
*If Domitian **were** still **ruling** us, **we should be** very unhappy.*

Further examples:

1 sī soror mea nunc vīveret, tē adiuvāret.
2 sī mīlitēs vōs in itinere comitārentur, minus sollicitus dē vōbīs essem.

2c *in the present tense of the subjunctive,* referring to FUTURE time:
sī hanc medicīnam *bibās*, statim *convalēscās*.
*If **you were to drink** this medicine, **you would get better** at once.*

sī piscēs per aera *volent*, omnēs *mīrentur*.
*If fish **were to fly** through the air, everyone **would be amazed**.*

Further examples:

1 sī imperātōrem occīdere cōnēris, ipse statim interficiāris.
2 pater meus, sī cognōscat quid fēcerim, mē sevērissimē pūniat.

2d *in two different tenses of the subjunctive (pluperfect and imperfect),* referring to a mixture of PAST and PRESENT time:
nisi mē *invēnissēs*, etiam nunc ibi *stārem*.
*If **you hadn't found** me, **I should** still **be standing** there now.*

25 Indirect Speech

1 *summary of differences between direct and indirect speech*

	direct	indirect
question	*"quid facis?"*	rogāvī hominem *quid faceret.*
	"What are you doing?"	*I asked the man what he was doing.*
command	*"pugnāte!"*	dux iuvenibus imperāvit *ut pugnārent.*
	"Fight!"	*The leader ordered the young men to fight.*
statement	*"poēta recitat."*	puer dīcit *poētam recitāre.*
	"A poet is reciting."	*The boy says that a poet is reciting.*

2 *indirect questions*, expressed by a question-word such as **quis** *who* or **num** *whether*,[*] followed by a subjunctive form of the verb:[†]

senex nesciēbat *quis templum aedificāvisset.*
The old man did not know who had built the temple.

(Compare this with the direct question: **quis templum aedificāvit?**)

mē rogāvērunt *num satis pecūniae habērem.*
They asked me whether I had enough money.

(Compare: **satis pecūniae habēs?**)

in animō volvēbam *quid māter dictūra esset.*
I was wondering what my mother would say, or was going to say.

(Compare: *"**quid māter dīcet?**"* and for further examples of this use of the future participle, see **7d**.4.)

necne is used in indirect questions to mean *or not*:
incertī erant utrum dux vīveret *necne.*
They were unsure whether their leader was alive or not.

(Compare: *"**utrum dux vīvit annōn?**"*)

Further examples:

1 magister scīre vult quis fenestram frēgerit.
2 puella hominem rogāvit quot piscēs cēpisset.
3 incertī sumus quārē cīvēs ad templum prōgrediantur.
4 dux nesciēbat quid hostēs factūrī essent.
5 cognōscere cōnābar num fēmina marītum occīdisset.

---

[*] For examples of **num** used (with a different meaning) in *direct* questions, see **11**.6.

[†] A question-word and subjunctive can also be used with such verbs as **rogō, scio, nescio**, etc. to express *indirect deliberative questions*. (Direct deliberative questions are described in **11**.7.) For example, **nesciēbam** *quid facerem* could mean either *I didn't know what I was doing* (indirect question) or *I didn't know what to do* (indirect deliberative question). Usually the context of the sentence makes it clear what the speaker means; if it doesn't, the speaker can make the meaning clear by using a different form of words (e.g. the gerundive, as described in **26**.2b, **nesciēbam** *quid faciendum esset I didn't know what ought to be done*).

3 *indirect commands,** usually expressed by **ut** or **nē** followed by a subjunctive form in the present or imperfect tense:

rēx mīlitibus imperāvit *ut captīvōs līberārent.*
The king ordered the soldiers *that they should set the prisoners free.*
Or, in more natural English:
The king ordered the soldiers **to set the prisoners free.**

(Compare this with the direct command: "**captīvōs līberāte!**")

puella mercātōrem ōrāvit *ut pecūniam redderet.*
The girl begged the merchant **to give the money back.**

(Compare: "**pecūniam redde!**")

lēgātus barbarōs hortātus est *ut mōrēs Rōmānōs discerent.*
The governor encouraged the barbarians **to learn Roman ways.**

(Compare: "**mōrēs Rōmānōs discite!**")

ab amīcīs monēmur *nē haruspicibus crēdāmus.*
We are advised by friends **not to believe the soothsayers.**

(Compare: "**nōlīte haruspicibus crēdere!**")

Indirect commands introduced by the verbs **iubeō** and **vetō** are expressed not by **ut** or **nē** and the subjunctive but by the infinitive:

domina servum iussit fenestram *reficere.*
The mistress ordered the slave **to repair** *the window.*

spectātōrēs vetābantur *cibum bēstiīs dare.*
The spectators were forbidden **to feed** *the animals.*
Or, *The spectators were told not* **to feed** *the animals.*

Further examples:

1 dominus ancillīs imperāvit ut vīnum ferrent.
2 agricola nōs monuit ut prīmā lūce proficīscerēmur.
3 sacerdōs puerōs vetuit in templō loquī.
4 amīcī mihi persuādēre cōnantur nē in hōc oppidō maneam.
5 senex nautam hortābātur ut nāvem vēnderet et tabernam emeret.

---

* Indirect commands can be introduced not only by verbs meaning "I order," "I demand," etc., but also by verbs meaning "I beg," "I persuade," "I request," "I warn," etc.

4 *indirect statements,* normally expressed by a noun or pronoun in the accusative case and an infinitive form of the verb:

4a *introduced by a verb in the present or future tense*

4b *introduced by a verb in a past tense*

with the present active infinitive

crēdō prīncipem **Agricolae**
invidēre.
I believe the emperor **to be jealous** of Agricola.

Or, in more natural English:
I believe that the emperor **is jealous** of Agricola.

crēdēbam prīncipem **Agricolae**
invidēre.
I believed the emperor **to be jealous** of Agricola.

Or, in more natural English:
I believed that the emperor **was jealous** of Agricola.

▌ (Compare these with the direct statement: "**prīnceps Agricolae invidet.**")

with the present passive infinitive

scit **multās prōvinciās ā latrōnibus** *vexārī.*

sciēbat **multās prōvinciās ā latrōnibus** *vexārī.*

He knows that many provinces **are troubled** by bandits.

He knew that many provinces **were troubled** by bandits.

▌ (Compare: "**multae prōvinciae ā latrōnibus vexantur.**")

with the perfect active infinitive

centuriō hostēs *dīcit cōnstitisse.*
The centurion **says** that the enemy **have halted.**

centuriō hostēs *dīxit cōnstitisse.*
The centurion **said** that the enemy **had halted.**

▌ (Compare: "**hostēs cōnstitērunt.**")

with the perfect passive infinitive

vir uxōrem *servātam esse putat.*
The man **thinks** that his wife **has been saved.**

vir uxōrem *servātam esse putāvit.*
The man **thought** that his wife **had been saved.**

▌ (Compare: "**uxor servāta est.**")

with the future active infinitive

senātōrēs *prō certō habent* **cīvēs numquam** *cessūrōs esse.*
The senators **are sure** that the citizens **will never give in.**

senātōrēs *prō certō habēbant* **cīvēs numquam** *cessūrōs esse.*
The senators **were sure** that the citizens **would never give in.**

▌ (Compare: "**cīvēs numquam cēdent.**")

with the future infinitive passive

captīvōs *interfectum īrī* **nūntiat.**
He **is announcing** that the prisoners **will be killed.**

captīvōs *interfectum īrī* **nūntiābat.**
He **was announcing** that the prisoners **would be killed.**

▌ (Compare: "**captīvī interficientur.**")

4c   Indirect statements introduced by verbs meaning "I hope," "I promise," "I threaten," etc. are normally expressed in Latin by an accusative and future infinitive (whereas English usually prefers a shorter form):

spērō *mē ventūrum esse.*
I hope that I shall come.
Or, in more natural English: *I hope to come.*

pollicitī sunt *sē discessūrōs esse.*
They promised that they would go away.
Or, in more natural English: *They promised to go away.*

4d   Forms of **sē, suus**, and **is** are used in the following ways in indirect statements:

Marcus dīcit sē in Britanniā habitāre.
Marcus says that he (i.e. Marcus) *lives in Britain.*

Marcus dīcit eum in Britanniā habitāre.
Marcus says that he (i.e. someone else) *lives in Britain.*

agricolae affirmāvērunt vīllās suās incēnsās esse.
The farmers claimed that their (i.e. the farmers') *villas had been burnt.*

agricolae affirmāvērunt vīllās eōrum incēnsās esse.
The farmers claimed that their (i.e. other people's) *villas had been burnt.*

4e   **negō** *I deny, I say that . . . not* is used in the following way:

iuvenis negāvit sē pecūniam perdidisse.
The young man denied that he had wasted the money.
Or, *The young man said that he had not wasted the money.*

Further examples:

1   servus dīcit ingentem nāvem portuī appropinquāre.
2   omnēs cīvēs crēdēbant Claudium venēnō necātum esse.
3   mercātor spērābat sē magnās dīvitiās in Hispāniā comparātūrum esse.
4   senātōrēs sciunt bellum terribile contrā Britannōs gerī.
5   audiō decem hominēs herī damnātōs esse.
6   amīcus meus putat urbem mox captum īrī.
7   homō clāmābat tabernam suam ardēre.
8   testis negāvit eum senī umquam nocuisse.
9   polliceor mē fenestram crās refectūrum esse.
10 fēmina suspicābātur puerum mentīrī.

5 For examples of different types of word order involving indirect speech
and verbs meaning "I ask," "I order," "I say," etc., see **28**.4.

6 Sometimes the verb which means "I ask," "I order," "I say," etc. is
omitted altogether, especially if one sentence in indirect speech is
followed immediately by another. The use of the accusative and
infinitive (or of the subjunctive) makes it clear that indirect speech is
being used. For example:

> **rēx dīxit Rōmānōs exercitum parāvisse; mox prīmōs mīlitēs
> adventūrōs esse.**
> *The king said that the Romans had prepared an army;* (he said that)
> *the first soldiers would soon arrive.*

The verb **dīxit** is not repeated in the second part of the sentence,
because the use of the accusative (**prīmōs mīlitēs**) and infinitive
(**adventūrōs esse**) makes it clear that the sentence is still reporting what
the king said.

> **fēmina marītum monuit ut domō quam celerrimē discēderet;
> proficīscerētur ante prīmam lūcem; mīlitēs eum quaerere.**
> *The woman warned her husband to leave the house as quickly as possible;*
> (she warned that) *he should set out before dawn;* (she said that)
> *soldiers were looking for him.*

The verb **monuit** is not repeated in the second part of the sentence,
because the use of the subjunctive (**proficīscerētur**) makes it clear that
the sentence is still reporting the woman's warning; and in the last part
of the sentence the accusative (**mīlitēs**) and infinitive (**quaerere**) make
it clear that this is a further report of what the woman said.

7 In indirect speech, the verb in a subordinate clause is normally
subjunctive:

> **mercātor respondit servōs quī vīnum *effunderent* magnō pretiō
> ēmptōs esse.**
> *The merchant replied that the slaves who **were pouring** out the wine had
> been bought at a high price.*

(Compare this with the direct statement: "**servī quī vīnum *effundunt*
magnō pretiō ēmptī sunt.**")

> **spectātōrēs affirmant Milōnem victūrum esse, quod cotīdiē sē
> *exerceat*.**
> *The spectators claim that Milo will win, because **he trains** every day.*

(Compare: "**Milō vincet, quod cotīdiē sē *exercet*.**")

26 Uses of the Gerund, Gerundive, and Supine

1 *gerund* (**portandum** *carrying,* **docendum** *teaching,* etc.), used in the
following cases:

accusative with **ad** (meaning "for the purpose of . . .")
   multī hominēs ad *audiendum* aderant.
   *Many men were there for the purpose of **listening**.*
Or, in more natural English:
   *Many men were there to **listen**.*

genitive
   optimam habeō occāsiōnem *cognōscendī* quid acciderit.
   *I have an excellent opportunity **of finding out** what has happened.*

dative
   operam *scrībendō* dedit.
   *He gave his attention **to writing**.*

ablative
   prūdenter *emendō* et *vēndendō*, pater meus dīvitissimus factus est.
   ***By buying** and **selling** sensibly, my father became very rich.*

Further examples:
1 trēs mīlitēs tabernam ad bibendum ingressī sunt.
2 omnēs hominēs dēbent artem bene dīcendī discere.
3 ancilla tua, fidēliter decem annōs serviendō, lībertātem meruit.
4 iūdex mihi nūllam occāsiōnem respondendī dedit.
5 puerī senem clāmandō vexāvērunt.

2 *gerundive* (**portandus, docendus,** etc.):

2a *meaning "being carried," "being taught," etc.,* used in the following cases:

accusative with **ad**
   iuvenis ad epistulam *legendam* cōnsēdit.
   *The young man sat down for the purpose of the letter **being read**.*
Or, in more natural English:
   *The young man sat down **to read** the letter.*

genitive
   nāvis *servandae* causā, magnam mercis partem in mare ēiēcērunt.
   *For the sake of the ship **being saved**, they threw a large part of the cargo overboard.*
Or, in more natural English:
   To save the ship, they threw a large part of the cargo overboard.

dative
   mīlitēs omnem operam armīs *parandīs* dabant.
   *The soldiers were giving all their attention **to preparing** their weapons.*

ablative
   custōdibus *dēcipiendīs*, ē carcere effūgī.
   ***By deceiving** the guards, I escaped from the prison.*

Further examples:

1 frāter meus in rīpā flūminis sedēre solēbat, ad piscēs capiendōs.
2 Caesar artem bellī gerendī bene sciēbat.
3 fabrī omnem operam templō perficiendō dabant.
4 amīcīs servandīs, centuriō magnam glōriam adeptus est.
5 avārus occāsiōnem pecūniae recipiendae āmīsit.

2b *meaning "needing to be carried," "needing to be done," etc.*, often used in the nominative case with some form of the verb **sum** and known as the *gerundive of obligation*:

discipulī *interrogandī* sunt.	*The students are **needing to be questioned**.*
	Or, in more natural English:
	*The students **must be questioned**.*

The dative is used to indicate the person who has to do the action:

longum iter mihi *faciendum* erat.* *I had to make a long journey.*
vīlla nōbīs *aedificanda* est.* *We **must build** a villa.*
mīlitibus *cōnsistendum* erit.* *The soldiers **will have to halt**.*

Further examples:

1 flammae exstinguendae sunt.
2 in hōc locō nōbīs pugnandum est.
3 nāvis tibi reficienda est.
4 servīs dīligenter labōrandum erat.
5 fundus mihi vēndendus erit.

3   *supine* (**portātum, doctum**, etc.) used in the following cases:

accusative, used with verbs involving movement, indicating purpose:
cīvēs *dormītum* abiērunt.
*The citizens went away **to sleep**.*

The accusative of the supine is also used with **īrī** (present passive infinitive of **eō** *I go*) to form the future passive infinitive:

nūntius dīcit vīllam *dēlētum* īrī.
*The messenger says that **there is a movement (īrī) to destroy** the villa.*
Or, in more natural English:
*The messenger says that the villa **will be destroyed**.*

ablative, used with certain adjectives:
mōnstrum terribile *vīsū* erat.
*The monster was terrible **to see**.*

---

* Sentences like these cannot be translated literally into natural English. For example, the literal translation of **longum iter mihi faciendum erat** would be something like *There was a long journey for me, needing to be made,* which sounds so peculiar that it must be rephrased as *I had to make . . . etc.*

PART THREE

WORD ORDER AND SENTENCE STRUCTURE

27 Word Order in Short Sentences

(examples of some common patterns and ways in which they can be varied)

1 *sentences consisting of a nominative noun and verb*

   1a *nominative + verb*
   custōdēs dormiēbant.   *The guards were asleep.*

   1b *verb + nominative*
   dēcidit rēx.   *The king fell down.*
        Or, *Down fell the king.*

2 *sentences consisting of two nouns (nominative and accusative) and a verb*

   2a *nominative + accusative + verb* (an extremely common word order)
   cīvēs templum vīsitābant.   *The citizens were visiting the temple.*

   2b *verb + accusative + nominative*
   dedit signum haruspex.   *The diviner gave the signal.*
        Or, *It was the diviner who gave the signal.**

      A Roman could use this word order to emphasize **haruspex**. For example, he might guess that his readers (or listeners) would expect the signal to be given by the trumpeter, not by the diviner, and he might therefore choose to hold back the word **haruspex** so that the sentence ends with a surprise.

   2c *accusative + nominative + verb*
   equum agricola vēndidit.   *The farmer sold the horse.*
        Or, *What the farmer sold was the horse.*

      This word order could be used by a Roman who has just been asked "What did the farmer sell?"; he might choose to start his reply with **equum** because it gives the answer to the question. Another reason for beginning with **equum** might be to emphasize a contrast with some other animal; for example, **equum . . . vēndidit** might be followed by **porcum retinuit**, *The farmer sold the horse but kept the pig.*

---

*Other translations (of this and other sentences) are also possible, e.g. *The person who gave the signal was the diviner.*

3 *sentences containing three nouns (nominative, accusative, and dative) and a verb*

3a *nominative + dative + accusative + verb* (a common order)
mīles puerō gladium ostendit. *The soldier showed his sword to the boy.*

3b *dative + nominative + accusative + verb*
uxōrī mercātor nihil lēgāvit. *The merchant left nothing to his wife.*
Or, *To his wife the merchant left nothing.*

> One of the reasons for which a writer might use this word order is to emphasize a contrast between **uxōrī** and another word. For example, **uxōrī . . . lēgāvit** might be followed by **libertīs vīllam ingentem**, *To his wife the merchant left nothing, but to his freedmen he left an enormous villa.*

3c *accusative + verb + nominative + dative*
grātiās ēgērunt cōnsulēs *The consuls thanked the slaves.*
servīs. Or, *The people whom the consuls thanked were the slaves.*

> In this sentence, **servīs** is placed last (a rather unusual position for a dative). There are various reasons why a writer might choose to do this. For example, instead of emphasizing the fact that the consuls thanked anyone, he might want to emphasize that the ones who were thanked were (perhaps unexpectedly) the slaves.

4 Further examples of all the patterns in paragraphs 1–3:

1 iuvenēs clāmōrem faciēbant.
2 intrāvit senex.
3 māter fīliō dōnum ēmit.
4 ancillās iūdex laudāvit.
5 praemium dedit dominus coquō.
6 centuriōnēs proficīscēbantur.
7 senātōribus spectātōrēs omnia nārrāvērunt.
8 interfēcit lupum Sextus.

5 *sentences which do not contain nominatives*

5a *accusative + verb*
candidātum salūtāvērunt. *They greeted the candidate.*

5b *dative + verb*
amīcīs crēdidit. *He believed his friends.*

5c *dative + accusative + verb*
nūntiō epistulam trādidī. *I handed a letter to the messenger.*

Further examples:

1 iānuam aperuērunt.
2 hospitibus vīnum offerēbam.
3 nāvem reficiēbāmus.
4 deae cōnfīdēbat.
5 patrī dēnāriōs reddidī.
6 captīvīs pepercērunt.

28 Word Order in Longer Sentences

1 *relative clauses*

1a *following main clause*
prope āram stābant mīlitēs, *quī dūcem custōdiēbant.*
*Near the altar stood the soldiers, **who were guarding the leader.***

1b *in middle of main clause*
uxor mea, *quae strepitum audīverat*, statim accurrit.
*My wife, **who had heard the din***, *came running up at once.*

equum *quem āmīseram* repperī.
*I found the horse **that I had lost.***

1c *in front of main clause* (normally with forms of **is** or **īdem** as the antecedent):
***quī tē heri culpābat*, is tē hodiē laudat.**
*The person **who was blaming you yesterday** is praising you today.*

***quae tibi coniūnx est*, eadem mihi fīlia paene est.**
*The same woman **who is a wife to you** is virtually a daughter to me.*

***quae dominus iussit*, ea servōs efficere oportet.**
What the master has ordered, *the slaves must carry out.*
Or, *The slaves must carry out **what the master has ordered.***

Sometimes the antecedent is omitted altogether:
quod potuī*, fēcī.**   *I have done **what I could.
***quī audet*, vincit.**   *He **who dares**, wins.*

Further examples:

1 ancillae, quibus domina magnum praemium prōmīserat, dīligenter labōrābant.
2 mercātor duōs coquōs ēmit, quōrum alter Graecus, alter Aegyptius erat.
3 quod rēx vōbīs heri dedit, id vōbīs crās auferet.
4 custōdēs quī dormīverant sevērissimē pūnīvī.
5 quī semper haesitat, nihil umquam efficit.

2 *other subordinate clauses and phrases containing participles*

    2a *following main clause*
    spectātōrēs vehementer clāmāvērunt, *quod īrātissimī erant.*
    *The spectators shouted loudly, **because they were very angry.***

    in mediō ātriō sedēbat pontifex maximus, *togam splendidam gerēns.*
    *In the middle of the hall sat the chief priest, **wearing a splendid toga.***

    2b *in middle of main clause*
    medicus, *dum cēnat,* **ad cubiculum prīncipis arcessītus est.**
    ***While the doctor was dining,** he was summoned to the emperor's bedroom.*

    2c *in front of main clause*
    simulac rēx signum dedit, **equitēs hastās coniēcērunt.**
    ***As soon as the king gave the signal,** the horsemen threw their spears.*

Further examples:

1 Caesar praecōnī imperāvit ut nōmen victōris recitāret.
2 mīlitēs, undique circumventī, dē vītā dēspērābant.
3 quamquam nox erat obscūra, viaeque dēsertae, puella nōn timēbat.

3 *two or more subordinate clauses or phrases containing participles*

    3a *leading out of the main clause, and placed one after the other*
    dominus incertus erat *quō fūgisset servus, cūr abesset coquus, quot dēnāriī ablātī essent.*
    *The master was uncertain **where the slave had fled to, why the cook was missing, and how many denarii had been stolen.***

    3b *one leading out of the other, and placed after it*
    puerī timēbant, *quod prope iānuam iacēbat ingēns canis, vehementer lātrāns.*
    *The boys were afraid **because near the door was lying a huge dog, barking loudly.***

    3c *one inside the other*
    ubi ā culīnā in quā cēnāverat redībat, **centuriōnem cōnspexit.**
    ***When he was returning from the kitchen in which he had been dining,** he caught sight of the centurion.*

Further examples:

1 fūr, cum ad cubiculum ubi senex dormīre solēbat pervēnisset, in līmine cōnstitit.
2 lēgātus mox cognōvit ubi hostēs castra posuissent, quot mīlitēs in castrīs essent, quis mīlitibus praeesset.
3 deōs precāta ut fīlium suum tūtum redūcerent, fēmina ē templō exiit.

4 *verbs meaning "I ask," "I order," "I say," etc.*

4a *in front of indirect speech*
ducem ōrābant nē vīllam incenderet. (*indirect command*)
They were begging *the leader not to set fire to the villa.*

haruspicēs *cognōscent* **num ōmina bona sint.** (*indirect question*)
The diviners **will find out** *whether the omens are good.*

nūntius *respondit* **multa oppida dēlēta esse.** (*indirect statement*)
The messenger **replied** *that many towns had been destroyed.*

4b *in middle of indirect speech*
multōs hospitēs *audiō* **invītārī.**
I **hear** *that many guests are being invited.*

4c *following indirect speech*
utrum custōs esset an carnifex, nēmō *sciēbat.*
Whether he was a guard or an executioner, no one **knew.**

iuvenem pecūniam redditūrum esse *cōnfīdimus.*
We are sure *that the young man will give the money back.*

māter puerōs nē silvam intrārent identidem *monuit.*
The mother repeatedly **warned** *the boys not to go into the wood.*

Further examples:

1 cognōscere voluī quārē senex catēnīs vīnctus esset.
2 amīcum nostrum suspicābāmur nimis vīnī bibisse.
3 hospitēs senātōrī ut loquī dēsineret tandem persuāsērunt.
4 quot equitēs captī sint, incertum est.
5 medicus Claudium venēnō necātum esse crēdēbat.

29 Noun and Adjective Phrases

1 *noun and adjective*

multus sanguis	*much blood*
vir benignus	*a kind man*

Adjectives which indicate size or quantity (e.g. **magnus, multī**) are usually placed before the noun they describe; other adjectives are usually placed after. But the Romans did not observe this as a strict rule.

2 *noun and adjective separated by a preposition*

mediīs in undīs	*in the middle of the waves*
hanc ad tabernam	*to this shop*

3 *noun and adjective separated by one word or more* (this and the following patterns are particularly common in poetry)

nox erat, et *caelō* **fulgēbat lūna** *serēnō*. *(Horace)*
It was night, and the moon was shining in a **clear sky.**

4 *two pairs of noun and adjective phrases, one following the other*

atque *opere* **in** *mediō laetus* **cantābat** *arātor*.
And the **happy plowman** *was singing in the* **middle of his work.**

5 *two pairs of noun and adjective phrases, one inside the other*

agna *lupōs* **audit circum** *stabula alta frementēs*. *(Ovid)*
The lamb hears the **wolves howling** *around the* **tall sheepfolds.**

6 *two pairs of noun and adjective phrases, intertwined*

cantātur *tōtā nōmen* **in** *urbe meum*.
My name *is sung* ***all over the city.***

The following type of intertwining is known as the "golden line":

1st adjective + 2nd adjective + verb + 1st noun + 2nd noun

parvula **nē** *nigrās* **horrēscat** *Erōtion umbrās* *(Martial)*
for fear that **little Erotion** *should shudder at the* **dark shadows**

7 Further examples of the patterns described in paragraphs 4–6:

1 *Midday in summer*
in *mediō caelō Phoebus* **iam** *fervidus* **ardet.**

2 *The rapid building of Rome's city wall*
et *novus exiguō tempore mūrus* **erat.** *(Ovid)*

3 *A courageous young sailor*
nōn timet *ingentēs iuvenis fortissimus undās*.

4 *A workman is promised a hot bath*
fessaque **mox** *calidā membra* **lavābis** *aquā*.

calidus *hot*	membrum *limb*
exiguus *small, short*	Phoebus *Phoebus Apollo*, i.e. *the sun*
fervidus *intense, fierce*	

30 Omission of Words from Sentences

1   *omission of forms of* **sum** (e.g. *est, erat,* etc.)
    iam hōra diēī prīma.   *Now it was the first hour of the day.*

> (Compare this with a longer way of expressing the same idea:
> **iam hōra diēī prīma** *erat.*)

multī occīsī, rēx captus.   *Many were killed and the king was captured.*

> (Compare: **multī occīsī** *sunt,* **rēx captus** *est.*)

sē dēceptum sēnsit.   *He realized he had been deceived.*

> (Compare **sē dēceptum** *esse* **sēnsit.**)

2   *omission of forms of* **is** *as antecedents of* **quī**
    quod suscēpī, effēcī.   *I have carried out what I undertook.*

> (Compare: **quod suscēpī,** *id* **effēcī,** or, *id* **quod suscēpī, effēcī.**)
> For further examples, see **28.**1c.

3   *omission of word from one of two clauses*

3a   *word omitted from second clause*
     Britannī cibum laudāvērunt, Rōmānī vīnum.
     The Britons praised the food, the Romans praised the wine.

> (Compare: **Britannī cibum laudāvērunt, Rōmānī vīnum** *laudāvērunt.*)

plūrimī spectātōrēs gladiātōrem incitābant, nōnnūllī leōnem.
Most spectators were encouraging the gladiator, some were encouraging the lion.

> (Compare: **plūrimī spectātōrēs gladiātōrem incitābant, nōnnūllī leōnem** *incitābant.*)

3b   *word omitted from first clause*
     sacerdōs templum, poēta tabernam quaerēbat.
     The priest was looking for a temple, the poet (was looking) for an inn.

> (Compare: **sacerdōs templum** *quaerēbat,* **poēta tabernam quaerēbat.**)

et movet ipse suās et nātī respicit ālās.
He both moves his own wings himself and looks back at those of his son.

> (Compare: **et ipse suās** *ālās* **movet et ālās nātī respicit.**)
> See also **40.**25

Further examples:
1 iuvenis taurum dūcēbat, puella equum.
2 sī dōnum Imperātōris recūsābis, stultus eris; sī accipiēs, prūdēns.
3 aliī pecūniam, aliī glōriam petunt.
4 haec est statua illīus deae, quam Britannī Sūlem, Rōmānī Minervam vocant.

PART FOUR

MISCELLANEOUS

31 How to Use a Latin–English Dictionary*

1 *nouns* (and some pronouns) are normally listed in the following way:
nominative singular : genitive singular : gender[†] : meaning

So, if the following information is given:
pāx, pācis, f. *peace*
pāx means "peace," **pācis** means "of peace," and the word is
feminine.

The genitive singular always shows the declension to which a noun
belongs, and so can be used (together with a table of nouns if
necessary, such as the ones in **1**.1–5) to identify the case or cases
indicated by a particular ending.

Example 1a : **dominus**
dictionary entry : dominus, dominī, m. *master*
This shows that **dominus** is a second-declension noun (like **servus**,
shown in **1**.2) and so **dominus** must be nominative singular.

Example 1b : **corpus**
dictionary entry : corpus, corporis, n. *body*
This shows that **corpus** is a third-declension noun (like **tempus**, **1**.3)
and so **corpus** is either nominative or vocative or accusative singular.

Example 1c : **aedificium**
dictionary entry : aedificium, aedificiī, n. *building*
This shows that **aedificium** is a second-declension noun (like **templum**,
1.2) and so **aedificium** is either nominative or vocative or accusative
singular.

Example 1d : **montium**
dictionary entry : mōns, montis, m. *mountain*
This shows that **mōns** is a third-declension noun (like **urbs**, **1**.3) and so
montium must be genitive plural, meaning "of the mountains."

---

* All Latin-English dictionaries follow the general plan described in this
  section, though they sometimes differ from each other slightly in small
  details of layout, etc.
† The abbreviation "pl." after the gender indicates that the noun is normally
  used only in its plural forms. For example,
  castra, castrōrum, n.pl. *camp*

Example 1e : **piscī**
dictionary entry : piscis, piscis, m. *fish*
This shows that **piscis** is a third-declension noun (like **cīvis**, **1**.3) and so **piscī** must be dative singular, meaning "to a fish."

Example 1f : **amīcī**
dictionary entry : amīcus, amīcī, m. *friend*
This shows that **amīcus** is a second-declension noun (like **servus**, **1**.2) and so **amīcī** is either genitive singular ("of a friend") or nominative or vocative plural.

Exercise Use a dictionary (and, if necessary, the tables in 1.1–5) to identify the cases of the following:

1 auctōrī	3 populō	5 capitis
2 hortī	4 virgō	6 silvīs

2 *adjectives of the first and second declension* (and most pronouns) are normally listed in the following way:

nominative masculine singular : nominative feminine singular : nominative neuter singular : meaning

So, if the following information is given:
    superbus, superba, superbum *proud*
superbus is the masculine form, **superba** the feminine, and **superbum** the neuter, of the nominative singular.
Sometimes only endings are listed, e.g. **superb-us, -a, -um**.

3 *adjectives of the third declension* are normally listed in one of the following ways:

(i) nominative masculine singular : nominative feminine singular : nominative neuter singular : meaning

So, if the following information is given:
    ācer, ācris, ācre *eager, excited*
ācer is the masculine, **ācris** the feminine, and **ācre** the neuter form, of the nominative singular.

(ii) nominative masculine and feminine singular : nominative neuter singular : meaning

So, if the following information is given:
    fortis, forte *brave*
fortis is the masculine and feminine, and **forte** the neuter form, of the nominative singular.

(iii) nominative singular (all genders) : genitive singular (all genders) : meaning

So, if the following information is given:
    ferōx, ferōcis *fierce* (sometimes with *"gen."* before the genitive)
ferōx is the nominative singular, and **ferōcis** the genitive singular, of all three genders.

4   *verbs* are usually listed in the following way:

the 1st person singular of the present tense;
the infinitive;
the 1st person singular of the perfect tense;
the supine;
the meaning.

So, if the following information is given:
    pōnō, pōnere, posuī, positum *place*
pōnō means "I place," **pōnere** means "to place," **posuī** means "I placed" and **positum** is the supine (whose use is described in **26**.3).

These four forms are known as the *principal parts* of a verb. All the forms of a normal verb can be identified if its principal parts are known (supplemented if necessary by reference to tables of verbs, such as those in **7 – 9**). The supine is not often met, but is used in forming some very important parts of the verb, such as the perfect passive participle. For example, **positus** *having been placed* is formed from the supine **positum**.*

Example 4a : **neglexistī**
dictionary entry : neglegō, neglegere, neglexī, neglēctum *neglect*
This shows that **neglexistī** is from the perfect tense of **neglegō** and so means "you (singular) neglected."

Example 4b : **monitus erat**
dictionary entry : moneō, monēre, monuī, monitum *advise, warn*
This shows that **monitus erat** is from the pluperfect passive of **moneō** and so means "he had been advised, warned."

The principal parts, listed in the dictionary, can be used to check which conjugation a verb belongs to, and thus translate its tense correctly.

Example 4c : **iubet**
dictionary entry : iubeō, iubēre, iussī, iussum *order*
This shows that **iubeō** is a *second*-conjugation verb (like **doceō**, shown in **7**) and so **iubet** must be a *present* tense and means "he orders."

---

* If a verb has no supine and no perfect passive participle, only the first three principal parts are usually listed.

Example 4d : **dūcet**
dictionary entry : dūcō, dūcere, dūxī, ductum *lead*
This shows that **dūcō** is a *third*-conjugation verb (like **trahō** in **7**) and so **dūcet** must be a *future* tense and means "he will lead."

Exercise Use a dictionary (and, if necessary, the tables in **7**) to identify the tenses of the following, then translate them:

1 exercet	3 cōgētis	5 prohibēmur
2 scindet	4 persuādētis	6 mittēmur

5   *deponent verbs* are listed in the following way:

the 1st person singular of the present tense;
the infinitive;
the 1st person singular of the perfect tense;
the meaning.

So, if the following information is given:
     sequor, sequī, secūtus sum *follow*
sequor means "I follow," **sequī** means "to follow," and **secūtus sum** means "I followed."

The principal parts, listed in the dictionary, can be used to check whether a word with a passive ending (e.g. **ēgrediuntur, custōdiuntur**) comes from a deponent verb or not.

Example 5a : **ēgrediuntur**
dictionary entry : ēgredior, ēgredī, ēgressus sum *go out*
It is clear from the listed forms that **ēgredior** is a *deponent* verb; **ēgrediuntur** must therefore have an *active* meaning, i.e. "they go out."

Example 5b : **custōdiuntur**
dictionary entry : custōdiō, custōdīre, custōdīvī, custōdītum *guard*
It is clear from the listed forms that **custōdiō** is *not* a deponent verb; **custōdiuntur** must therefore have a *passive* meaning, i.e. "they are being guarded."

Exercise Translate the following, using a dictionary to check whether they are deponent verbs or not, and referring if necessary to the tables in **7** and **8**:

1 sequitur	3 vocābar	5 ingressī sunt
2 relinquitur	4 mīrābar	6 oppressī sunt

6   Verbs used with a direct object (see **14.5a**), e.g. **laudō**, are known as *transitive* verbs, indicated in many dictionaries by *tr.*; verbs used without a direct object, e.g. **currō**, are known as *intransitive* verbs, indicated by *intr.*

7 Adjectives and verbs used with the genitive, dative, or ablative cases
are indicated by +*gen.*, +*dat.* and +*abl.* respectively.

8 Prepositions used with the accusative case, such as *trāns*, are indicated
by +*acc.*; those used with the ablative, such as *ex*, are indicated by
+*abl.*

9 Some Latin words can be spelled in more than one way. In particular,
verbs beginning with such prefixes as **ab-, ad-, con-, in-** or **sub-**, followed
by a consonant, sometimes change the last letter of the prefix for ease of
pronunciation (e.g. **inpellō** can become **impellō**, **abferō** always becomes
auferō, **adtollō** is usually spelled **attollō**, and **conlocō, collocō**), or drop
the last letter of the prefix altogether (e.g. **adspiciō** is usually spelled
aspiciō).

So (for example),
words not listed with the spelling **adc** . . . may be listed under **acc** . . .

"	"	"	**adf** . . .	"	"	**aff** . . .
"	"	"	**adg** . . .	"	"	**agg** . . .
"	"	"	**adl** . . .	"	"	**all** . . .
"	"	"	**adp** . . .	"	"	**app** . . .
"	"	"	**adsc** . . .	"	"	**asc** . . .
"	"	"	**adsp** . . .	"	"	**asp** . . .
"	"	"	**conl** . . .	"	"	**coll** . . .
"	"	"	**conm** . . .	"	"	**comm** . . .
"	"	"	**inl** . . .	"	"	**ill** . . .
"	"	"	**inm** . . .	"	"	**imm** . . .
"	"	"	**inp** . . .	"	"	**imp** . . .
"	"	"	**inr** . . .	"	"	**irr** . . .
"	"	"	**subm** . . .	"	"	**summ** . . .

and vice versa.

32 List of Predicative Datives

Almost any noun has a dative form, but not every noun is common as
a predicative dative, used with a form of **sum**. The following nouns are
frequently used as predicative datives and often appear with a dative
of the person concerned, the so-called dative of interest. For the double
dative construction with **sum**, see **14.4c**.

adiūmentō	*(be) a help*	decōrī	*(be) an ornament*
admīrātiōnī	*(be) a surprise*	dēdecorī	*(be) a disgrace*
argūmentō	*(be) a proof*	dētrīmentō	*(be) a detriment*
auxiliō	*(be) a help*	documentō	*(be) a lesson*
bonō	*(be) a benefit*	dolōrī	*(be) a grief*
calamitātī	*(be) a disaster*	dōnō	*(be) a gift*
causae	*(be) a cause/reason*	ēmolumentō	*(be) an advantage*
crīminī	*(be) a reproach*	exemplō	*(be) an example*
cūrae	*(be) a care/burden*	exitiō	*(be) a ruin*
damnō	*(be) an injury*	fraudī	*(be) a deceit*

frūctuī	*(be) a satisfaction*	praesidiō	*(be) a protection*
glōriae	*(be) a boast*	probrō	*(be) a shame*
honōrī	*(be) an honor*	pudōrī	*(be) a cause for shame*
impedīmentō	*(be) a hindrance*	quaestuī	*(be) a profit*
laudī	*(be) a merit*	religiōnī	*(be) a moral obligation*
lucrō	*(be) a profit*	remediō	*(be) a cure*
lūdibriō	*(be) a mockery*	salūtī	*(be) a deliverance*
malō	*(be) an evil*	sōlāciō	*(be) a comfort*
mūnerī	*(be) a duty*	subsidiō	*(be) a help*
odiō	*(be) hateful*	sūmptuī	*(be) an expense*
onerī	*(be) a burden*	terrōrī	*(be) a dread*
opprobriō	*(be) a disgrace*	testimōniō	*(be) evidence*
ōrnāmentō	*(be) an ornament*	timōrī	*(be) an alarm*
perīculō	*(be) a danger*	ūsuī	*(be) useful*
pignorī	*(be) a security*	vitiō	*(be) a fault*
praedae	*(be) plunder*	voluptātī	*(be) a pleasure*

33 List of Adjectives with Special Cases

1 *adjective + genitive*

affīnis	*connected with* (also frequently with dative)
aliēnus	*unsuitable for/alien from* (also frequently with dative or ablative)
amāns	*lover of*
appetēns	*desirous of*
avidus	*covetous of*
capāx	*capable of*
cōnscius	*conscious of*
cupidus	*fond of*
dīligēns	*careful of*
dissimilis	*different from* (also frequently with dative)
edāx	*devouring of*
expers	*destitute of*
expertus	*experienced in*
gnārus	*skilled in*
ignārus	*unskilled in/ignorant of*
immemor	*unmindful of*
imperītus	*inexperienced in*
inānis	*void of*
incertus	*uncertain of*
inexpertus	*inexperienced in*
inops	*destitute of*
īnscius	*ignorant of*
manifestus	*convicted of*
memor	*mindful of*
patiēns	*tolerant of*

perītus	*experienced in*
plēnus	*full of* (also frequently with ablative)
prūdēns	*knowing of*
refertus	*filled full of* (also frequently with ablative)
reus	*bound by*
rudis	*ignorant of*
similis	*similar to* (also frequently with dative)
studiōsus	*fond of*
tenāx	*grabbing hold of*
vacuus	*empty of*

2 *adjective + dative*

affīnis	*related to* (also frequently with genitive)
aliēnus	*alien from/unsuitable for* (also frequently with genitive or ablative)
amīcus	*friendly to*
aptus	*suited to* (also frequently with **ad** + accusative)
cārus	*dear to*
commūnis	*common to* (also frequently with genitive)
dissimilis	*dissimilar to* (also frequently with genitive)
fidēlis	*faithful to*
grātus	*pleasing to*
idōneus	*suitable for* (also frequently with **ad** + accusative)
impār	*unequal to*
īnfēnsus	*hostile to*
īnfestus	*dangerous for*
inimīcus	*unfriendly to*
inūtilis	*useless to*
iūcundus	*pleasing to*
obnoxius	*addicted to/submissive to*
obvius	*open to*
pār	*equal to* (also less frequently with genitive)
proprius	*peculiar to* (also with genitive)
proximus	*nearest to*
sacer	*consecrated to*
similis	*similar to* (also frequently with genitive)
superstes	*surviving* (also frequently with genitive)
ūtilis	*useful to*
vīcīnus	*neighboring to*

3 *adjective + ablative*

aliēnus	*alien from/unsuitable for* (also frequently with genitive or dative)
contentus	*content with*
dignus	*worthy of*
frētus	*relying on*
immūnis	*unburdened by*
indignus	*unworthy of*
līber	*free from*
nūdus	*deprived of*
orbus	*deprived of*
plēnus	*filled with/full of* (also frequently with genitive)
praeditus	*furnished with*
pūrus	*undefiled by*
refertus	*filled full of* (also frequently with genitive)
solūtus	*loosened from*
vacuus	*free from*

34 List of Verbs with Special Cases

1 *impersonal verbs.* Number in parentheses identifies the type of conjugation (1st, 2nd, 3rd, 4th, or irregular). See also **19**.1.

1a *impersonal verbs describing weather*

fulgurat (1)	*it is lightening* (cf. **fulgor** *lightning*)
grandinat (1)	*it is hailing* (cf. **grandō** *hail*)
lūcēscit (3)	*it is beginning to shine/it is growing light* (cf. **lūx** *light*)
ningit (3)	*it is snowing* (**nix** *snow*)
pluit (3)	*it is raining* (cf. **pluvia** *rain*)
tonat (1)	*it is thundering* (cf. **tonitrus** *thunder*)
(ad-)vesperāscit (3)	*it is twilight* (cf. **vesper** *evening*)

1b *impersonal verbs + genitive + accusative*

miseret (2)	*it makes (one) feel pity because of*
paenitet (2)	*it makes (one) regret because of*
piget (2)	*it vexes (one) because of*
pudet (2)	*it makes (one) ashamed because of*
taedet (2)	*it makes (one) tired because of*

1c *impersonal verbs + accusative*

decet (2)	*it suits (one)*
dēdecet (2)	*it does not suit (one)/it is a disgrace to (one)*
dēlectat (1)	*it delights (one)/(one) is delighted*
iuvat (1)	*it pleases (one)/(one) is pleased*
oportet (2)	*it is right for (one)/(one) ought*

1d *impersonal verbs + dative + infinitive*

abest (irr.)	*it is disadvantageous for (one) to . . .*
condūcit (3)	*it is advantageous for (one) to . . .*
convenit (4)	*it is proper for (one) to . . .*
displicet (2)	*it displeasing to (one) to . . .*
expedit (4)	*it is expedient for (one) to . . .*
libet (2)	*it is agreeable to (one) to . . .*
licet (2)	*it is permitted to (one) to . . .*
placet (2)	*it is pleasing to (one) to . . .*
prōdest (irr.)	*it is beneficial for (one) to . . .*
vidētur (2)	*it seems good to (one) to . . .*

1e *impersonal verbs + (dative) + consecutive "ut" -clause*

(tibi) accidit (3) ut eās	*it happens that you are going/you happen to be going*
(tibi) contingit (3) ut eās	*it falls to your lot that you are going/ you happen to be going*
(tibi) ēvenit (4) ut eās	*it comes to pass that you are going*
(tibi) fierī (irr.) potest ut eās	*it can happen that you are going/ you may be going*
(tibi) fit (irr.) ut eās	*it happens that you are going*

1f *other impersonal verbs*

accēdit (3)	*it befalls*	liquet (2)	*it is clear*
appāret (2)	*it is apparent*	patet (2)	*it is obvious*
attinet (2)	*it concerns*	pertinet (2)	*it suits*
cōnstat (1)	*it is agreed*	praestat (1)	*it is preferable*
fallit (3)	*it deceives*	rēfert (irr.)	*it is important*
fugit (3)	*it escapes*	restat (1)	*it remains*
interest (irr.)	*it is important*	tantum abest (irr.)	*it is so far from*

1g *impersonal expressions with neuter noun + form of "sum"*

cōnsilium est	*have a plan*
necesse est	*must*
opus est	*have business with/need for*
tempus est	*be the time to/for*

2 *verbs frequently with genitive.* Number in parentheses identifies the type of conjugation (1st, 2nd, 3rd, 4th, or irregular).

absolvō (3)	*absolve/acquit from*
(in-)accūsō (1)	*(not) blame because of/accuse of*
admoneō (2)	*put in mind of*
arcessō (3)	*accuse of*
arguō (3)	*accuse of*
commonefaciō (3)	*remind of*

(con-)damnō (1)	*judge guilty of/sentence*
egeō (2)	*be in need of* (also frequently with ablative)
indigeō (2)	*be in need of/not have enough of* (also frequently with ablative
meminī	*be mindful of/remember*
mentiōnem faciō (3)	*make mention of*
misereor (2)	*feel pity because of/feel pity for*
miserēscō (3)	*feel pity because of/feel pity for*
miseret (2)	*it makes (one) feel pity because of*
oblīvīscor (3)	*be forgetful of*
paenitet (2)	*it makes (one) regret because of*
piget (2)	*it vexes (one) because of*
postulō (1)	*accuse of*
potior (4)	*be master of* (also frequently with ablative)
pudet (2)	*it makes (one) ashamed because of*
reminīscor (3)	*be reminded of*
taedet (2)	*it makes (one) tired because of*

3 *verbs frequently with dative.* Number in parentheses identifies the type of conjugation (1st, 2nd, 3rd, 4th, or irregular).

appropinquō (1)	*come near to*
cōnfīdō (3)	*put trust in*
crēdō (3)	*have faith in*
displiceō (2)	*be displeasing to*
faveō (2)	*show favor to*
ignōscō (3)	*be forgiving to*
imperō (1)	*give an order to*
indulgeō (2)	*be indulgent to*
invideō (2)	*be jealous towards*
noceō (2)	*be harmful to*
nūbō (3)	(original meaning probably) *put on the marriage-veil for*
obstō (1)	*be an obstacle to*
parcō (3)	*be merciful to*
pāreō (2)	*be obedient to*
persuādeō (2)	*be persuasive to*
placeō (2)	*be pleasing to*
resistō (3)	*put up a resistance to*
serviō (4)	*be a slave for*
studeō (2)	*be devoted to*

and many compound verbs, e.g.

| praesum (irr.) | *be the commander for* |
| subveniō (4) | *come as a rescuer for* |

4 *Verbs frequently with ablative.* Number in parentheses identifies the type of conjugation (1st, 2nd, 3rd, or 4th).

abstineō (2)	*keep back from*
abundō (1)	*be rich in*
aliēnō (1)	*estrange from*
arceō (2)	*keep away from*
careō (2)	*be without*
cēdō (3)	*withdraw from*
cessō (1)	*cease from*
compleō (2)	*fill with*
cumulō (1)	*pile with*
dēsistō (3)	*desist from*
dignor (1)	*deem worthy of*
dōnō (1)	*present with*
egeō (2)	*be in need of* (also frequently with genitive)
fraudō (1)	*cheat out of*
fruor (3)	*derive enjoyment from/enjoy*
(dē-)(per-)fungor (3)	*busy oneself with/perform*
glōrior (1)	*pride oneself on/brag about*
indigeō (2)	*be in need of* (also frequently with genitive)
levō (1)	*alleviate with*
līberō (1)	*deliver from*
moveō (2)	*move from*
nītor (3)	*support oneself with/lean on*
onerō (1)	*burden with*
opus est	*there is need for*
orbō (1)	*deprive of*
pellō (3)	*drive away from*
potior (4)	*be enriched with/be master of* (also frequently with genitive)
prīvō (1)	*deprive of*
referciō (4)	*stuff with*
solvō (3)	*remove from*
temperō (1)	*regulate with*
(ab-)ūtor (3)	*serve oneself with/use*
vacō (1)	*be without*
vēscor (3)	*feed upon*

35 Summary of Subjunctive Uses*

1 *in main clauses*

1a *deliberative questions* (described in **11**.7):
quid *dīcam?*   *What **am I** to say?*
utrum *pugnēmus* **an** *fugiāmus? **Should we fight** or **run away?***

1b *jussive subjunctive* (**12**.3):
lūdōs *spectēmus!*   ***Let us watch** the games!*
epistulam statim *recitet.*   ***Let him read out** the letter at once.*
     Or, ***He is to read out** the letter at once.*

1c *wishes* (**13**):
utinam *mānsissēs!*   *If **only you had stayed**!*
utinam nē *capiātur!*   ***May he not get caught**!*

1d *in the main clause of some types of conditional sentence* (**24**.2):
mercātor, sī *circumspectāvisset, fūrem vīdisset.*
*If the merchant **had looked round**, he **would have seen** the thief.*

A subjunctive form of the verb is also used in the main clause of
sentences that *imply* a conditional clause without actually *stating* it:

tū ipse eīs *crēderēs. You yourself **would believe** (or **would have believed**)*
     them (implying a conditional clause, e.g. "if you
     had been there," "if you had heard them," etc.)
aliquis hoc *dīcat,*   Someone may say this . . . (implying, e.g., "if he
     dīxerit . . .   wants to," "if he disagrees with me," etc.)

This is sometimes described as the *potential* use of the subjunctive. The
pluperfect tense is used to refer to past time; the imperfect tense can refer
to either present or past time; the present and (sometimes) perfect tenses
are used to refer to future time.

Further examples:

1 loquar an taceam?
2 ad forum festīnēmus!
3 utinam iuvenis patrī pāruisset!
4 quō modō hostibus resistāmus?
5 sī servī aquam celeriter attulissent, domus flammīs nōn dēlēta esset.

---

* For further examples of each use, see the paragraph referred to under each
sub-heading.

2 *in subordinate clauses*

2a *purpose clauses* (**23**.2):
hīc manēbō, *ut* **vīllam** *dēfendam.*
I shall stay here to defend the villa.

prīnceps Plīnium ēmīsit *quī* **Bīthȳnōs** *regeret.*
The Emperor sent Pliny out to rule the Bithynians.

tacēbāmus, *nē* **ā centuriōne** *audīrēmur.*
We kept quiet, in order not to be heard by the centurion.

2b *result clauses* (**23**.3):
barbarī tot hastās coniēcērunt *ut* **plūrimī equitēs** *vulnerārentur.*
The barbarians threw so many spears that most horsemen were wounded.

2c *causal clauses* with **cum** *since* or with **quod** or **quia** to quote a reason
put forward by some other person or people (**23**.4):
cum **clientēs meī** *sītis,* **subveniam vōbīs.**
Since you are my clients, I will help you.

agricola fīlium castīgāvit *quod* **plaustrum reficere nōn** *cōnātus*
    esset.
The farmer scolded his son for not trying to mend the cart.

2d *temporal clauses* with **cum** *when*, and with **priusquam, antequam,
dōnec**, and **dum** to indicate purpose as well as time (**23**.5):
cum **prōvinciam** *circumīrem,* **incendium Nīcomēdīae coortum est.**
When I was going around the province, a fire broke out at Nicomedia.

abībō, *priusquam* **ā dominō** *agnōscar.*
I shall go away, before I am recognized by my master.

2e *concessive clauses* with **quamvīs** or **cum** *although* (**23**.6):
quamvīs **multōs librōs** *lēgerit,* **nihil didicit.**
Although he has read many books, he has learned nothing.

2f *comparative clauses*, making a comparison with an imaginary event
or situation (**23**.7):
per forum cucurrit *quasi* **ā leōne** *agitārētur.*
He ran through the forum as if he were being chased by a lion.

2g *clauses of fear or danger* (**23**.8):
verēbāmur *nē* **omnēs nāvēs** *dēlētae essent.*
We were afraid lest all the ships had been destroyed.
Or, in more natural English:
We were afraid that all the ships had been destroyed.

perīculum est *nē* **occīdāris.**
There is a risk that you may be killed.

2h *conditional clauses* in conditional sentences whose translation includes "would" (**24**.2):

sī dīves *essem*, nōn hīc habitārem.
If I were rich, I wouldn't be living here.

frāter meus, sī *certāvisset*, cēterōs facile vīcisset.
If my brother had competed, he would easily have beaten the others.

2j *indirect questions* (**25**.2):
centuriō cognōscere vult *ubi* barbarī *cōnstiterint*.
The centurion wants to find out where the barbarians have halted.

2k *indirect commands* (**25**.3):
tē moneō *ut* lēgibus *pāreās*.
I advise you to obey the laws.

medicus nōbīs imperāvit *nē ingrederēmur*.
The doctor told us not to go in.

2m *subordinate clauses inside indirect speech* (**25**.7):
testis affirmāvit latrōnēs, postquam mercātōrem vehementer *pulsāvissent*, pecūniam rapuisse.
The witness declared that the robbers, after they had hit the merchant violently, had seized his money.

Further examples:
1 tam saevus erat leō ut nēmō eī appropinquāre audēret.
2 cum dux mīlitēs īnstrūxisset, tuba sonuit.
3 custōdēs mē rogāvērunt quārē cōnsulem vīsitāre vellem.
4 māter puerīs imperāvit nē verba obscēna in mūrō scrīberent.
5 ad aulam contendimus ut veniam ā rēge peterēmus.
6 claudite portās castrōrum, priusquam hostēs intrent!
7 fabrī meī, quamvīs fessī sint, labōrāre nōn dēsinunt.
8 puella dīxit haruspicēs, postquam victimam īnspexissent, ōmina pessima nūntiāvisse.
9 servī laudābantur quia dominum ē perīculō servāvissent.
10 agricola attonitus cōnstitit, quasi porcum volantem cōnspicātus esset.
11 mercātor nāvem condūxit, quae frūmentum Rōmam veheret.
12 amīcī iuvenī persuāsērunt ut imperātōrem necāre cōnārētur.
13 sī pompam spectāvissētis, omnēs dēlectātī essētis.
14 valdē timēbam nē frāter meus ā iūdice damnārētur.

In each sentence, find the reason why a subjunctive is being used.

3 The tense of a subjunctive verb in a Latin subordinate clause depends on:

(i) the meaning, and

(ii) the tense of the verb in the main clause of the sentence, in accordance with the following rule, known as the rule of *sequence of tenses*:

If the verb in the main clause of the sentence is in a *primary* tense, i.e. present, future, perfect (meaning "have . . .," e.g. **portāvī** *I have carried*) or future perfect, the tense of the subjunctive must normally be *present* or *perfect* (or, in indirect questions, present subjunctive of **sum** with a future participle);

If the verb in the main clause is in a *historical* (sometimes known as *secondary*) tense, i.e. imperfect, perfect (meaning ". . .ed," e.g. **portāvī** *I carried*) or pluperfect, the tense of the subjunctive must normally be *imperfect* or *pluperfect* (or, in indirect questions, imperfect subjunctive of **sum** with a future participle).

The following table summarizes the various possible combinations of tense:

PRIMARY	**rogō**	*I ask*		**scrībat**	*he is writing*
	rogābō	*I shall ask*	**eum quid**	**scrīpserit**	*he has written*
	rogāvī	*I have asked*	*him what*	**scrīptūrus**	*he will write*
	rogāverō	*I shall have asked*		**sit**	
HISTORICAL	**rogābam**	*I was asking*		**scrīberet**	*he was writing*
	rogāvī	*I asked*	**eum quid**	**scrīpsisset**	*he had written*
	rogāveram	*I had asked*	*him what*	**scrīptūrus esset**	*he would write*

36 Principal Parts* of Some Common Verbs

Including examples (indented) of verbs extended by prefixes to form compound[†] verbs. Verbs which have similar ways of forming their 3rd or 4th principal parts are grouped together within each conjugation; so are deponent verbs:

1   *first conjugation*

    1a portō, portāre, portāvī, portātum *carry*

        Many other first-conjugation verbs form their principal parts in the same way as **portō**. For example:

        amō, amāre, amāvī, amātum *love*
        labōrō, labōrāre, labōrāvī, labōrātum *work*
        pugnō, pugnāre, pugnāvī, pugnātum *fight*
        rogō, rogāre, rogāvī, rogātum *ask*

    1b secō, secāre, secuī, sectum *cut*
        vetō, vetāre, vetuī, vetitum *forbid*

    1c iuvō, iuvāre, iūvī, iūtum *help*
        lavō, lavāre, lāvī, lautum (*sometimes* lavātum) *wash*

    1d dō, dare, dedī, datum *give*[§]
        stō, stāre, stetī, statum *stand*
        adstō, adstāre, adstitī *stand by*
        similarly: circumstō *stand around*; obstō *stand in the way*, etc.

    1e *deponent verbs*
        cōnor, cōnārī, cōnātus sum *try*
        hortor, hortārī, hortātus sum *encourage*
        minor, minārī, minātus sum *threaten*
        moror, morārī, morātus sum *delay*
        precor, precārī, precātus sum *pray (to)*

2   *second conjugation*

    2a moneō, monēre, monuī, monitum *advise, warn*

        Many other second-conjugation verbs form their principal parts in the same way as **moneō**. For example:

        dēbeō, dēbēre, dēbuī, dēbitum *owe, ought*
        exerceō, exercēre, exercuī, exercitum *practice, exercise*
        habeō, habēre, habuī, habitum *have*
            prohibeō, prohibēre, prohibuī, prohibitum *prevent*
        terreō, terrēre, terruī, territum *frighten*

---

*For explanations of the term "principal parts," see **31**.4 and **31**.5.
†For an explanation of the spelling of some of these forms, see **31**.9.
§For examples of compounds of *dō*, see **36**.3p.

2b doceō, docēre, docuī, doctum *teach*
teneō, tenēre, tenuī, tentum *hold*
retineō, retinēre, retinuī, retentum *hold back*

2c compleō, complēre, complēvī, complētum *fill*
dēleō, dēlēre, dēlēvī, dēlētum *destroy*
fleō, flēre, flēvī, flētum *weep*

2d augeō, augēre, auxī, auctum *increase*
fulgeō, fulgēre, fulsī *shine*

2e ardeō, ardēre, arsī *be on fire*
haereō, haerēre, haesī, haesum *stick, cling*
iubeō, iubēre, iussī, iussum *order*
maneō, manēre, mānsī, mānsum *remain*
rīdeō, rīdēre, rīsī, rīsum *laugh, smile*
suādeō, suādēre, suāsī, suāsum *advise*
persuādeō, persuādēre, persuāsī, persuāsum *persuade*

2f caveō, cavēre, cāvī, cautum *beware*
faveō, favēre, fāvī, fautum *favor, support*
moveō, movēre, mōvī, mōtum *move*

2g respondeō, respondēre, respondī, respōnsum *reply*

2h sedeō, sedēre, sēdī, sessum *sit*
obsideō, obsidēre, obsēdī, obsessum *besiege*
videō, vidēre, vīdī, vīsum *see*
invideō, invidēre, invīdī, invīsum *envy*

2j *deponent verbs*
polliceor, pollicērī, pollicitus sum *promise*
vereor, verērī, veritus sum *be afraid*
videor, vidērī, vīsus sum *seem*

2k *semi-deponent verbs*
audeō, audēre, ausus sum *dare*
gaudeō, gaudēre, gāvīsus sum *rejoice*
soleō, solēre, solitus sum *be accustomed*

2m Many of the verbs used impersonally which are listed in **19**.1 and **34**.1 belong to the second conjugation, with a 3rd person singular present indicative ending in **-et** and a perfect ending in **-uit**. For example:

pudet mē   *it makes me ashamed, I am ashamed*
puduit mē   *it made me ashamed, I was ashamed*

3   *third conjugation*

3a trahō, trahere, trāxī, tractum *drag*

Many other third-conjugation verbs form their principal parts in the same way as **trahō**. For example:

dīcō, dīcere, dīxī, dictum *say*
dūcō, dūcere, dūxī, ductum *lead*
    circumdūcō, circumdūcere, circumdūxī, circumductum *lead around*
    prōdūcō, prōdūcere, prōdūxī, prōductum *lead forward*
    similarly: abdūcō *lead away;* ēdūcō *lead out;* indūcō *lead in;* redūcō *lead*
        back, etc.
intellegō, intellegere, intellēxī, intellēctum *understand*
iungō, iungere, iūnxī, iūnctum *join*
regō, regere, rēxī, rēctum *rule*
    surgō, surgere, surrēxī, surrēctum *rise, get up*

3b gerō, gerere, gessī, gestum *wear, carry*
nūbō, nūbere, nūpsī, nūptum *marry*
scrībō, scrībere, scrīpsī, scrīptum *write*
sūmō, sūmere, sūmpsī, sūmptum *take*
    cōnsūmō, cōnsūmere, cōnsūmpsī, cōnsūmptum *eat*

3c cēdō, cēdere, cessī, cessum *give way*
    discēdō, discēdere, discessī, discessum *depart*
    prōcēdō, prōcēdere, prōcessī, prōcessum *advance*
    similarly: accēdō *approach;* incēdō *march;* recēdō *withdraw,* etc.
claudō, claudere, clausī, clausum *close*
laedō, laedere, laesī, laesum *hurt, harm*
lūdō, lūdere, lūsī, lūsum *play*
mittō, mittere, mīsī, missum *send*
    dīmittō, dīmittere, dīmīsī, dīmissum *send away, dismiss*
    ēmittō, ēmittere, ēmīsī, ēmissum *send out*
    similarly: āmittō *lose;* dēmittō *send down;* immittō *send in;*
        remittō *send back;* trānsmittō *send across,* etc.
plaudō, plaudere, plausī, plausum *applaud*
premō, premere, pressī, pressum *press*
    opprimō, opprimere, oppressī, oppressum *crush*
spargō, spargere, sparsī, sparsum *scatter*

3d bibō, bibere, bibī *drink*
comprehendō, comprehendere, comprehendī, comprehēnsum
    grasp, seize
dēfendō, dēfendere, dēfendī, dēfēnsum *defend*
incendō, incendere, incendī, incēnsum *burn*
scandō, scandere *climb*
    ascendō, ascendere, ascendī, ascēnsum *go up*
    dēscendō, dēscendere, dēscendī, dēscēnsum *go down*
scindō, scindere, scidī, scissum *tear*
vertō, vertere, vertī, versum *turn*
    animadvertō, animadvertere, animadvertī, animadversum *notice,*
    turn attention to

3e arcessō, arcessere, arcessīvī*, arcessītum *summon, send for*
    petō, petere, petīvī*, petītum *head for, attack; seek*
    quaerō, quaerere, quaesīvī*, quaesītum *look for, seek*

3f colō, colere, coluī, cultum *cultivate, worship*
    dēserō, dēserere, dēseruī, dēsertum *desert*
    pōnō, pōnere, posuī, positum *put*
       compōnō, compōnere, composuī, compositum *put together*
       prōpōnō, prōpōnere, prōposuī, prōpositum *put forward*
       similarly: circumpōnō *put around;* dēpōnō *put down;*
          expōnō *put out, explain;* impōnō *put into, put onto;*
          repōnō *put back,* etc.
    recumbō, recumbere, recubuī *lie down*

3g crēscō, crēscere, crēvī, crētum *grow*
    nōscō, nōscere, nōvī, nōtum *get to know*
       agnōscō, agnōscere, agnōvī, agnitum *recognize*
       cognōscō, cognōscere, cognōvī, cognitum *find out, get to know*
       ignōscō, ignōscere, ignōvī, ignōtum *forgive*
    sinō, sinere, sīvī, sītum *allow*
       dēsinō, dēsinere, dēsiī, dēsītum *stop, cease*
    spernō, spernere, sprēvī, sprētum *despise, reject*

3h agō, agere, ēgī, āctum *do, drive*
       cōgō, cōgere, coēgī, coāctum *force, compel*
    emō, emere, ēmī, ēmptum *buy*
    frangō, frangere, frēgī, frāctum *break*
    fundō, fundere, fūdī, fūsum *pour*
       effundō, effundere, effūdī, effūsum *pour out*
    legō, legere, lēgī, lēctum *read*
       colligō, colligere, collēgī, collēctum *gather*
       ēligō, ēligere, ēlēgī, ēlēctum *choose*
    relinquō, relinquere, relīquī, relictum *leave*
    rumpō, rumpere, rūpī, ruptum *break*
       corrumpō, corrumpere, corrūpī, corruptum *spoil, corrupt*
    vincō, vincere, vīcī, victum *conquer*

3j sistō, sistere, stitī *bring to a halt, make to halt*
       cōnsistō, cōnsistere, cōnstitī *stand still*
       dēsistō, dēsistere, dēstitī *stop, cease*
       resistō, resistere, restitī *resist*

3k metuō, metuere, metuī *fear*
    ruō, ruere, ruī *rush*
    solvō, solvere, solvī, solūtum *untie*
    statuō, statuere, statuī, statūtum *set up*
       cōnstituō, cōnstituere, cōnstituī, cōnstitūtum *decide*
       restituō, restituere, restituī, restitūtum *restore*
    volvō, volvere, volvī, volūtum *roll*

---

*sometimes shortened to **arcessiī, petiī** and **quaesiī**.

3m cadō, cadere, cecidī, cāsum *fall, die*
    accidō, accidere, accidī *happen*
    dēcidō, dēcidere, dēcidī *fall down*
  caedō, caedere, cecīdī, caesum *cut down, kill*
    occīdō, occīdere, occīdī, occīsum *kill*
  canō, canere, cecinī *sing*
  currō, currere, cucurrī, cursum *run*
    dēcurrō, dēcurrere, dēcurrī, dēcursum *run down*
    recurrō, recurrere, recurrī, recursum *run back*
    similarly: excurrō *run out;* incurrō *run in;* prōcurrō *run forward,* etc.
  discō, discere, didicī *learn*
  fallō, fallere, fefellī, falsum *deceive*
  parcō, parcere, pepercī *spare, be merciful*
  pellō, pellere, pepulī, pulsum *drive*
    expellō, expellere, expulī, expulsum *drive out*
    similarly: prōpellō *drive forward;* repellō *drive back,* etc.
  poscō, poscere, poposcī *demand*
  tangō, tangere, tetigī, tāctum *touch*
  tendō, tendere, tetendī, tentum *stretch*
    contendō, contendere, contendī, contentum *hurry*
    ostendō, ostendere, ostendī, ostentum *show*

3p* reddō, reddere, reddidī, redditum *give back*
  trādō, trādere, trādidī, trāditum *hand over*
  similarly: addō *add;* crēdō *believe;* ēdō *give out;* perdō *destroy, lose, waste;*
    prōdō *betray;* vēndō *sell,* etc.

3q *deponent verbs*
  adipīscor, adipīscī, adeptus sum *obtain*
  lābor, lābī, lāpsus sum *slip*
  loquor, loquī, locūtus sum *speak*
  nāscor, nāscī, nātus sum *be born*
  oblīvīscor, oblīvīscī, oblītus sum *forget*
  proficīscor, proficīscī, profectus sum *set out*
  queror, querī, questus sum *complain*
  sequor, sequī, secūtus sum *follow*
  ūtor, ūtī, ūsus sum *use*

3r *semi-deponent verbs*
  fīdō, fīdere, fīsus sum *trust*
    cōnfīdō, cōnfīdere, cōnfīsus sum *have confidence in, trust*
    diffīdō, diffīdere, diffīsus sum *distrust*

---

* The verbs in **36**.3p are all compounds of **dō** (which was shown in **36**.1d).
dō is a *first*-conjugation verb (infinitive **dare** with a short a), but nearly all its
compounds belong to the *third* conjugation (infinitives **reddere**, **trādere**,
etc.).

4   *third "-iō" conjugation*

4a capiō, capere, cēpī, captum *take, capture*
   accipiō, accipere, accēpī, acceptum *receive*
   suscipiō, suscipere, suscēpī, susceptum *undertake*
   similarly: dēcipiō *deceive*; incipiō *begin*; recipiō *recover*, etc.
  faciō, facere, fēcī, factum *do, make*
   efficiō, efficere, effēcī, effectum *carry out*
   praeficiō, praeficere, praefēcī, praefectum *put in charge*
   similarly: afficiō *affect*; cōnficiō *finish*; interficiō *kill*; obstupefaciō *amaze*;
       patefaciō *reveal*; reficiō *repair*, etc.
  fugiō, fugere, fūgī *flee, run away*
   effugiō, effugere, effūgī *escape*
  iaciō, iacere, iēcī, iactum *throw*
   abiciō, abicere, abiēcī, abiectum *throw away*
   dēiciō, dēicere, dēiēcī, dēiectum *throw down*
   similarly: coniciō *hurl*; ēiciō *throw out*; iniciō *throw in*; reiciō
       throw back, etc.

4b speciō, specere, spexī, spectum *see**
   circumspiciō, circumspicere, circumspexī, circumspectum *look around*
   respiciō, respicere, respexī, respectum *look back*
   similarly: aspiciō *look towards*; cōnspiciō *catch sight of*; dēspiciō *look down*;
       īnspiciō *inspect*, etc.

4c cupiō, cupere, cupīvī or cupiī, cupītum *desire*

4d rapiō, rapere, rapuī, raptum *seize*
   dīripiō, dīripere, dīripuī, dīreptum *tear apart, ransack*
   ēripiō, ēripere, ēripuī, ēreptum *snatch away*

4e *deponent verbs*
   gradior, gradī, gressus sum *go*
    aggredior, aggredī, aggressus sum *advance, attack*
    congredior, congredī, congressus sum *meet*
    similarly: ēgredior *go out*; ingredior *go in*;
          prōgredior *go forward*; regredior *go back*, etc.
   morior, morī, mortuus sum *die*
   patior, patī, passus sum *suffer*

5   *fourth conjugation*

5a audiō, audīre, audīvī*, audītum *hear*

   Many other fourth-conjugation verbs form their principal parts in the
   same way as **audiō**. For example:

   custōdiō, custōdīre, custōdīvī*, custōdītum *guard*
   dormiō, dormīre, dormīvī*, dormītum *sleep*
   impediō, impedīre, impedīvī*, impedītum *hinder*
   pūniō, pūnīre, pūnīvī*, pūnītum *punish*

---

* **speciō** itself is a fairly rare verb; but the compound verbs **circumspiciō,
respiciō**, etc. are very common.
* sometimes shortened to **audiī, custōdiī, dormiī**, etc.

5b reperiō, reperīre, repperī, repertum *find*
venīō, venīre, vēnī, ventum *come*
  adveniō, advenīre, advēnī, adventum *arrive*
  reveniō, revenīre, revēnī, reventum *come back*
  similarly: circumveniō *surround;* conveniō *come together, meet;*
    inveniō *come upon, find;* perveniō *reach;* subveniō *come to help,*
    etc.

5c aperiō, aperīre, aperuī, apertum *open*
salīō, salīre, saluī *jump*
  dēsiliō, dēsilīre, dēsiluī *jump down*

5d sentiō, sentīre, sēnsī, sēnsum *feel*
  cōnsentiō, cōnsentīre, cōnsēnsī, cōnsēnsum *agree*
  dissentiō, dissentīre, dissēnsī, dissēnsum *disagree*

5e sepeliō, sepelīre, sepelīvī*, sepultum *bury*

5f hauriō, haurīre, hausī, haustum *drain*
vinciō, vincīre, vīnxī, vīnctum *bind*

5g *deponent verbs*
mentior, mentīrī, mentītus sum *tell a lie*
orior, orīrī, ortus sum *arise*

6 *irregular*

6a eō, īre, iī *or* īvī, itum (other forms of this verb are listed in 9.1–3) *go*
exeō, exīre, exiī, exitum *go out*
trānseō, trānsīre, trānsiī, trānsitum *cross*
  similarly: abeō *go away;* adeō *go towards;* circumeō *go around;*
    pereō *perish;* redeō *return,* etc.

6b ferō, ferre, tulī, lātum (other forms in 9.1–3 and 9.5) *bring*
afferō, afferre, attulī, allātum* *bring along*
auferō, auferre, abstulī, ablātum *take away, steal*
efferō, efferre, extulī, ēlātum *bring out*
referō, referre, rettulī, relātum *bring back*
  similarly: circumferō *carry around;* īnferō *bring in;* offerō *offer,* etc.

6c fīō, fierī, factus sum (other forms in 9.1–4) *be made, become*

6d meminī, meminisse (other forms in 9.6) *remember*
ōdī, ōdisse (other forms in 9.6) *hate*

6e sum, esse, fuī (other forms in 9.1–3) *be*
absum, abesse, āfuī *be away, be absent*
possum, posse, potuī (other forms in 9.1–3) *be able*
praesum, praeesse, praefuī *be in charge*
  similarly: adsum *be present;* dēsum *be missing;* prōsum *be useful;*
    supersum *be left over, survive,* etc.

6f tollō, tollere, sustulī, sublātum *raise, remove*

6g volō, velle, voluī (other forms in 9.1–3) *want, be willing*
mālō, mālle, māluī (other forms in 9.1-3) *prefer*
nōlō, nōlle, nōluī (other forms in 9.1-3) *not want, refuse*

---

* For an explanation of the spelling of these and other forms of compounds of
ferō, see **31**.9.

37 Examples of Cognate Words

(i.e. words related to each other)

1a	*verb*		1b	*noun ending in -or*	
	amāre	*to love*		amor	*love*
	clāmāre	*to shout*		clāmor	*shout*
	labōrāre	*to work*		labor	*work*

2a	*adjective*		2b	*noun ending in -itūdō*	
	altus	*high, deep*		altitūdō	*height, depth*
	magnus	*great*		magnitūdō	*greatness, size*
	sōlus	*alone*		sōlitūdō	*loneliness, solitude*
	fortis	*brave*		fortitūdō	*bravery*
	multī	*many*		multitūdō	*crowd*

3a	*adjective*		3b	*noun ending in -ia*	
	amīcus	*friendly*		amīcitia	*friendship*
	superbus	*proud, arrogant*		superbia	*pride, arrogance*
	audāx	*bold*		audācia	*boldness*
	sapiēns	*wise*		sapientia	*wisdom*
	trīstis	*sad*		trīstitia	*sadness*

4a	*adjective*		4b	*noun ending in -tās*	
	benignus	*kind*		benignitās	*kindness*
	īnfirmus	*weak*		īnfirmitās	*weakness*
	līber	*free*		lībertās	*freedom*
	crūdēlis	*cruel*		crūdēlitās	*cruelty*
	gravis	*heavy, serious*		gravitās	*heaviness, seriousness*

5a	*verb (supine shown in parentheses)*		5b	*noun ending in -tor*	
	arāre (arātum)	*to plow*		arātor	*plowman*
	spectāre (spectātum)	*to watch*		spectātor	*watcher*
	dūcere (ductum)	*to lead*		ductor	*leader*
	vincere (victum)	*to win*		victor	*winner*

6a	*verb*		6b	*noun ending in -or*		6c	*adjective ending in -idus*	
	nitēre	*to shine*		nitor	*brightness*		nitidus	*bright, shining*
	pallēre	*to be pale*		pallor	*paleness*		pallidus	*pale*
	timēre	*to fear*		timor	*fear*		timidus	*fearful*

7a	*verb*		7b	*noun ending in -tiō*	
	coniūrāre	*to plot, conspire*		coniūrātiō	*plot, conspiracy*
	haesitāre	*to hesitate*		haesitātiō	*hesitation*
	salūtāre	*to greet*		salūtātiō	*greeting*
	quaerere	*to search, inquire*		quaestiō	*inquiry, investigation*
	scrībere	*to write*		scrīptiō	*writing*

8a *verb*
certāre	*to compete*
fluere	*to flow*
nōmināre	*to name*
impedīre	*to hinder*
vestīre	*to clothe, dress*

8b *noun ending in* **-men, -mentum**
certāmen	*contest*
flūmen	*river*
nōmen	*name*
impedīmentum	*hindrance*
vestīmentum	*clothing*

9a *verb* (supine shown in parentheses)
advenīre (adventum)	*to arrive*
cōnsentīre (cōnsēnsum)	*to agree*
redīre (reditum)	*to return*
monēre (monitum)	*to warn*
plaudere (plausum)	*to applaud*

9b *noun ending in* **-tus, -sus**
adventus	*arrival*
cōnsēnsus	*agreement*
reditus	*return*
monitus	*warning*
plausus	*applause*

10a *noun*
fōrma	*beauty, appearance*
līmus	*mud*
ōtium	*leisure, idleness*
perīculum	*danger*
pretium	*price, value*

10b *adjective ending in* **-ōsus**
fōrmōsus	*beautiful*
līmōsus	*muddy*
ōtiōsus	*idle, on holiday*
perīculōsus	*dangerous*
pretiōsus	*precious, valuable*

11a *verb*
aedificāre	*to build*
imperāre	*to order*
gaudēre	*to rejoice, be pleased*
studēre	*to study, be keen on*

11b *noun ending in* **-ium**
aedificium	*building*
imperium	*power*
gaudium	*joy*
studium	*study, enthusiasm*

12a *verb*
audēre	*to dare*
loquī	*to talk*
mentīrī	*to tell a lie*
pugnāre	*to fight*

12b *adjective ending in* **-āx**
audāx	*bold, daring*
loquāx	*talkative*
mendāx	*lying, deceitful*
pugnāx	*fond of fighting*

13a *noun*
cēna	*dinner*
culpa	*blame*
lacrima	*tear*
mora	*delay*
pugna	*fight*

13b *verb*
cēnāre	*to dine*
culpāre	*to blame*
lacrimāre	*to weep, cry*
morārī	*to delay*
pugnāre	*to fight*

117

14a *positive*

scīre	*to know*
volō	*I want*
umquam	*ever*
ōtium	*leisure*
amīcus	*friend*
fēlīx	*lucky*
ūtilis	*useful*
cōnsentīre	*to agree*
facilis	*easy*
similis	*like*

14b *negative*

nescīre	*not to know*
nōlō	*I do not want*
numquam	*never*
negōtium	*non-leisure, i.e. business*
inimīcus	*enemy*
īnfēlīx	*unlucky*
īnūtilis	*useless*
dissentīre	*to disagree*
difficilis	*difficult*
dissimilis	*unlike*

15a *noun*

homō	*man*
liber	*book*
servus	*slave*
cēna	*dinner*
vīlla	*country-house*

15b *diminutive*

homunculus	*little man*
libellus	*little book*
servulus	*little slave*
cēnula	*little dinner*
vīllula	*little country-house*

16a *masculine noun*

deus	*god*
dominus	*master*
fīlius	*son*
saltātor	*dancer (male)*
victor	*winner (male)*

16b *feminine noun*

dea	*goddess*
domina	*mistress*
fīlia	*daughter*
saltātrīx	*dancer (female)*
victrīx	*winner (female)*

For further examples of cognate words, see the list of adjectives in **33**, and the examples of compound verbs in **36**.

38 Notes on Pronunciation

1 *short vowels*

a	as in (American) English "**part**"
e	as in (American) English "**bet**"
i	as in (American) English "**grim**"*
o	as in (American) English "**obey**"
u	as in (American) English "**put**"
y	as in French "**plume**"†

Practice examples: **agit, bonus, lyricus, medius, pater**

---

* If "**i**" is followed by a vowel (e.g. in **iam**), it is being used as a consonant and is pronounced in the way described in paragraph 4.

†"**y**" was used by the Romans in certain words taken over from Greek; long and short "**y**" had the same pronunciation.

2 *long vowels* (marked with a macron (¯) in this and other reference books)

   ā   as in (American) English "'father'"
   ē   as in (American) English "they"
   ī   as in (American) English "machine"
   ō   as in (American) English "note"
   ū   as in (American) English "rude" (NOT as in "music")

Practice examples: **dē, fūr, māter, mīrābilis, tōtus**

3 *diphthongs* (two vowels sounded together in a single syllable)

   ae   as in (American) English "aisle"
   au   as in (American) English "out"
   ei   as in (American) English "vein"
   eu   no exact English equivalent: "e" is combined with "oo," in the
        same breath-impulse
   oe   as in (American) English "oil"
   ui   no exact English equivalent: "u" is combined with "i" in the
        same breath-impulse

Practice examples: **aeger, deinde, ēheu, foedus, huic, nauta**

4 *consonants*

   b   (usually) as in English "big"
   b   (followed by t or s) as in English "lips"
   c   as in English "cat" or "king" (NOT as in "center" or "cello")
   ch   as in English "cat" pronounced with emphasis ("You cat!")
        (NOT as in "chin")
   g   as in English "got" (NOT as in "gentle")
   gn   as "ngn" in English "hangnail"
   i   (sometimes written as j) as in English "you"
   n   (usually) as in English "net"
   n   (before c, g or qu) as in English "anger"
   ph   as in English "pig" pronounced with emphasis ("Pig!") (NOT as
        in "photo")
   qu   as in English "quick"
   r   as in French ("trilled") pronunciation of "fleur"
   s   as in English "sing" (NOT as in "roses")
   th   as in English "terrible' pronounced with emphasis ("Terrible!")
        (NOT as in "the" or "theater")
   v   (often written as u) as in English "wind"
   x   as in English "box"

Other consonants are pronounced as in English.

Practice examples: **caelum, chorus, cīvēs, Ephesus, fabrī, iānua,
ingēns, magnus, nūntius, obtineō, quī, regiō, rēx, theātrō, urbs, via**

119

5   *doubled consonants*

Both consonants are pronounced. For example:

ll   as in English "hall-light" (NOT as in "taller")
nn   as in English "thin-nosed" (NOT as in "dinner")
pp   as in English "hip-pocket" (NOT as in "happy")

Practice examples: **aggredior, annus, occupō, pessimus, supplicium, vīlla**

6   *finding syllables*

A syllable is a single uninterrupted sound unit within a word. For example, **audiāmus** *Let us listen!* contains four syllables, or sound units (**au-di-ā-mus**).
   The number of syllables in a Latin word equals the number of vowels or diphthongs in it. In a syllable, a vowel may be by itself or have a consonant(s) before and/or after it (e.g. **-ō** in **do-ce-ō, do-** or **ce-** in **do-ce-ō** or **spe-** in **spe-ci-ēs**, or **-ēs** in **spe-ci-ēs**, or **fert**).

6a   A consonant is pronounced with the vowel that follows it, e.g. **rogāvit (ro-gā-vit)** *s/he asked.*

6b   If two vowels or a vowel and diphthong appear together, pronounce them separately, e.g. **diēs (di-ēs)** *day,* **fīliae (fī-li-ae)** *daughters.*

6c   If two consonants appear together, pronounce them separately, e.g. **spectātor (spec-tā-tor)** *spectator,* **sollicitus (sol-li-ci-tus)** *worried.**

6d   If more than two consonants appear together, pronounce all except the last with the preceding vowel, and the last with the following vowel, e.g. **cūnctor, cūnc-tor.**

6e   If the word is compounded, pronounce its original parts separately, e.g. **cōnsūmit (cōn + sūmit,** then **cōn-sū-mit)** *s/he eats.*

7   *word stress* (indicated in this paragraph by an accent (´))

7a   In a word of two syllables, the stress falls on the first syllable, e.g. **ámō, ámās**, etc.

7b   In a word of three or more syllables, the stress falls on the second-syllable from the end if that syllable is *heavy* (i.e. contains (i) a long vowel, OR (ii) a diphthong, OR (iii) a short vowel followed by two consonants or **x** or **z**), e.g. **portámus, cōnféctus.**

7c   In all other words of three or more syllables, the stress falls on the third syllable from the end, e.g. **amīcítia, cōnspíciō.**

Practice examples: **amīcus, ancilla, equus, fīlius, leō, mercātor, monēbant, monent, rēgīna, sacerdōs, trahet.**

---

* A stop consonant (**b, p, d, t, g,** or **c**) followed by a liquid (**l** or **r**) is treated like a single consonant, e.g. **mōnstrum (mōns-trum)** *monster.*

39 Basic Metrics

1 *poetic beats of dactylic hexameter line*

Each line of Latin poetry is an arrangement of heavy (long) and light (short) syllables. Each arrangement carries its own pattern of poetic "beats" (in Latin, a poetic beat is called an "ictus"). Each word within an arrangement carries its own stress (**38**.7).

In the example below (with the arrangement of a dactylic hexameter), a beat is marked with a grave accent (ˋ), and a word stress with an acute accent (ˊ). Notice that sometimes the beat and the stress coincide (ˆ):

tûm míhi caèrúleùs súprà cáput âdstitit îmber.
"Then a blue raincloud stood over my head."

Vergil, *Aeneid* III.194

Read the above line aloud, emphasizing both the beats and word stresses. When a beat (ˋ) and stress (ˊ) coincide (ˆ) emphasize doubly hard.

2 *weight or "quantity" of syllables*

The arrangement of a line of Latin verse is based on a pattern of syllables (**38**.6) with long or short quantities.

A syllable is heavy (long) by nature (—) if it contains a long vowel or diphthong, e.g. **cae-** in **caē-rŭ-lĕ-ŭs** or **-rā** in **sup-rā**; and a syllable containing a short vowel is light (short) by nature (˘) e.g. **-rŭ-** and **-lĕ-** in **caē-rŭ-lĕ-ŭs**.

A syllable is heavy or "long by position" if it contains a short vowel followed by (1) two consonants, one of which may start the next word, e.g. **-us** and **sup-** in **caē-rŭ-lĕ-ūs súp-rā** (in prose: **caē-rŭ-lĕ-ŭs** and **sŭp-rā**) or (2) a double consonant (**x** or **z**), e.g. **-līx** in **īn-fē-līx**. (Note that a poet *may*, if he wishes, treat a stop consonant (**b, p, d, t, g,** or **c**) followed by a liquid (**l** or **r**) like a single consonant, but Vergil has not done so here in the **sūprā** of this line.)

A syllable is "doubtful" (i.e. it can be either light (short) or heavy (long) as the poet wishes) if it contains a short vowel followed by a stop consonant (**b, p, d, t, g,** or **c**) followed by a liquid consonant (**l** or **r**), e.g. **nēc** and **lăc-** in **nēc lăc-rĭ-mīs** "nor with tears" (Vergil, *Aeneid* V.173), or **ūt-** in **pāl-mās** . . . **ūt-rās-que** "stretching out both hands" (in prose: **ŭtrāsque**) (Vergil, *Aeneid* V.233).

3 *elision*

Drop (i.e. do not pronounce) (1) a vowel or diphthong at the end of a word before another word beginning with a vowel or **h**, e.g. **eumqu(e)** in **dīx-ĭt ĕ-ūm-qu' ī-mīs sūb flūc-ti-bŭs** "he spoke, and him beneath the lowest waves . . ." (Vergil, *Aeneid* V.239), or (2) a final **m** preceded by a vowel before another word beginning with a vowel or **h**, e.g. **imperi(um)** in **dī, quĭ-bŭs īmpĕ-rĭ' ēst** "the gods, to whom there is power" (Vergil, *Aeneid* V.235).

4 *scansion of dactylic hexameter*

To determine the poetic beat (ˋ) of a dactylic hexameter line, divide it into its component "feet" (|) on the following pattern (For help with finding syllables, see 38.6.):

‾˘˘ | ‾˘˘ | ‾˘˘ | ‾˘˘ | | ‾ -

or   or   or   or   ‾˘˘   or

‾ - | ‾- ˋ | ‾- | ‾- | | ‾˘

For example,

sō̄-lūs | iâmqu' íp- | sṑ sū́-pĕr- | èst ín | fî-nĕ Clŏ- | ân-thŭs,
And now Cloanthus alone is left at the very goal,

quêm pĕ́-tit | êt sŭ́m- | mìs ād- | nî-xūs | vî-rĭ-bŭs | ûr-gĕt.
whom [Mnestheus] heads for and presses, exerting
    himself with his utmost strength."

(Vergil, *Aeneid* V.225-26)

The poetic beat (ˋ) is carried on the first syllable of every foot. In the dactylic hexameter, therefore, there are six feet (|) with six beats (ˋ).

Exercises Mark the feet (|) and beats (ˋ) in each of the following dactylic hexameter lines:

īn - fē - līx sā - xīs īn prō - cūr - rēn - tĭ - bŭs haē - sĭt.
(Vergil, *Aeneid* V. 206)

cōn - sūr - gūnt nāū - t(ae) ēt māg - nō clā - mō - rĕ mŏ - rān - tŭr.
(Vergil, *Aeneid* V.207)

prō - nă pĕ - tit mă - rĭ(a) ēt pĕ - lă - gō dē - cūr - rĭt ă - pēr - tō.
(Vergil, *Aeneid* V.212)

hōr - tā - tūr - quĕ sĕ - quī, dām - nō - sās - qu(e) ē - rŭ - dĭt ār - tēs.
(Ovid, *Metamorphoses* VIII.215)

"Ī - că - rĕ," dī - xĭt, "ŭ - b(i) ēs? quā tē rĕ - gĭ - ō - nĕ rĕ - quī - răm?"
(Ovid, *Metamorphoses* VIII.232)

5 *caesura and diaeresis*

The ending of a word within a foot is called a caesura ("cut"). The ending of a word at the end of a foot is called a diaeresis ("divide"). The mark for either a caesura or diaeresis is (‖), e.g. īn-fē- | līx ‖ sā- | xīs ‖ (a caesura twice) and prō-nă pĕ- | tĭt ‖ mă-ri' ‖ (a caesura and a diaeresis).

6 *poetic beats of elegiac couplet*

The elegiac couplet comprises two lines, a dactylic hexameter alternating with a "pentameter" line, which is actually the first two-and-a-half feet of a hexameter twice.

To determine the poetic beat (ˋ) of an elegiac couplet, divide it into its component feet (|) on the following pattern (for help with finding syllables, see **38.6**):

(1) ´ ˇ ˇ | ´ ˇ ˇ | ´ ˇ ˇ | ´ ˇ ˇ | | ´ ‐

    or   or   or   or ´ ˇ ˇ or

    ´ ‐ | ´ ‐ | ´ ‐ | ´ ‐ | | ´ ˇ

      (2) ´ ˇ ˇ | ´ ˇ ˇ | ‖ | |

         or or   ´   ´ ˇ ˇ ´ ˇ ˇ   ´

           ´ ‐ | ´ ‐ |

For example,

âc – cĭ - pĕ | frā̀ - tér- | nò múl- | tùm mā- | nân- tĭ - ă | flê̂ - tū,
"Accept (my offerings) drenched with a brother's tears,

ât - qu(e)ˏín | pèr - pé - tŭ- | ùm, ‖ frā̂ - tĕr, á- | v(e)ˏât - quĕ vá- | lè.
and for ever, brother, hail and farewell."

                                 (Catullus, *Poems* CI.9-10)

Eù - trá - pĕ- | lùs tón- | sòr dúm | cîr - cŭ - ĭt | ô - rǎ Lŭ- | pêr - cī
"While Eutrapelus the barber goes around Lupercus' face,

èx - pīn- | gît - quĕ gé- | nàs, ‖ âl - tĕ - rǎ | bâr - bǎ súb- | ĭt.
and rouges his cheeks, another beard comes up."

                                 (Martial, *Epigrams* VII.83)

Exercise Mark the feet (|) and the beats (ˋ) in the following elegiac couplet:

ēx - ĭ - gĭs ūt nōs - trōs dō - nēm tĭ - bĭ, Tūc - că, lĭ - bēl - lōs.

nōn fǎ - cĭ - ām: nām vīs ‖ vēn - dĕ - rĕ, nōn lĕ - gĕ - rĕ.

                                 (Martial, *Epigrams* VII.77)

7   *poetic beats of hendecasyllabic line* (=11–syllable line)

The hendecasyllabic line is an arrangement of eleven syllables within five feet.

To determine the poetic beat (`) of a hendecasyllabic line, divide it into its component feet (|) on the following pattern (For help with finding syllables, see **38.**6.):

```
≟ -  |    |    |    |  ≟ _

or   ≟ ˇ ˇ   ≟ ˇ   ≟ ˇ   or

ˇ ≟  |    |    |    |  ≟ ˇ
```

For example,

pâs - sēr | môr - tŭ - ŭs | êst mé- | āê pŭ- | êl - lae,
"The sparrow of my girlfriend is dead,

pâs - sēr, | dè - lí - cĭ- | āê mé- | āê pŭ- | êl - lae,
the sparrow, the darling of my girlfriend,

quêm plús | îl - l(a) ő - cŭ- | lìs sú- | ìs ă- | mâ - băt.
whom she loved more than her own eyes."   (Catullus, *Poems* III.3-5)

Exercise Mark the feet (|) and the beats (`) in the following hendecasyllabic lines:

vī - vā - mūs, mě - ă Lēs - bi(a), āt - qu(e) ă - mē - mŭs.
                                                    (Catullus, *Poems* V.1)

mī - rā - rīs vě - tě - rēs, Vă - cēr - ră, sō - lōs

nēc lāū - dās nĭ - sĭ mōr - tŭ - ōs pŏ - ē - tās.
                                            (Martial, *Epigrams* VIII.69.1-2)

40 Figures of Speech

With examples from North American poets and from Vergil.

1   *alliteration* Repeating the same sound in two or more words, usually the first sound in the words.

The soul selects her own **society.**   *Emily Dickinson*

vāstō cum **murmure montis**
it **mare prōruptum** et **pelagō premit** arva sonantī.
"with a mighty mountain's rumble
it goes, a bursting sea, and overpowers the fields with a resounding flood."

                                            Vergil, *Aeneid* I.245-46

2 *anaphora* Repeating the same word/phrase at the beginning of successive clauses or phrases.

> "**Prophet!**" said I, "thing of evil! – **prophet** still, if bird or devil!"
>
> *Edgar Allan Poe*

> **nunc** augur Apollō
> **nunc** Lyciae sortēs, **nunc** et Iove missus ab ipsō
> interpres dīvum fert horrida iussa per aurās.
> "now the prophet Apollo
> now the Lycian oracles, now, sent by Jupiter himself,
> the messenger of the gods brought the frightful orders through the air."
>
> Vergil, *Aeneid* IV.376-78

3 *anastrophe* Reversal of usual order.

> **Time present** and **time past**
> Are both perhaps present in **time future**.   *T. S. Eliot*

> **quōs inter** medius vēnit furor.
> "Between whom hate arose in their midst."
>
> Vergil, *Aeneid* I.348

4 *aposiopesis* Sudden and deliberate "breaking off" in a clause.

> "**quamquam ō – sed superent, quibus hoc, Neptūne, dedistī.**"
> " 'Although, oh! – but let those win to whom you, Neptune, granted this.' "
>
> Vergil, *Aeneid* V.195

5 *assonance* Resemblance in sound, especially of the vowels in neighboring words.

> **Lonely**, **lovely**, and still, **Lonely**.   *William Cullen Bryant*
> O, **fellow**, **follow**.   *Delmore Schwartz*

> **omnibus** īdem **animus**, scelerātā excēdere terrā.
> "Everyone is of one mind, to leave that polluted land."
>
> Vergil, *Aeneid* III.60

> **mūgīre adytīs cortīna reclūsīs**
> The caldron (seemed) to roar from the sanctuary, now opened.
>
> Vergil, *Aeneid* III.92

6 *asyndeton* Omission of a conjunction(s).

Sawdust, spittoon, no smoking, please excuse.

Conrad Aiken

"feror exsul in altum
cum sociīs nātōque, **penātibus** et magnīs dīs."
" 'An exile, I am borne onto the deep
with my comrades and son, my household idols and the great gods.' "

Vergil, *Aeneid* III.11-12

7 *chiasmus* Repetition in the opposite order.

Hate-hardened heart, O heart of iron . . .

Marianne Moore, *In Distrust of Merits*

obstipuit simul ipse, **simul percussus** Achātēs
laetitiāque metūque.
"(Aeneas) himself was amazed and at the same time Achates (was)
overcome with both joy and fear."

Vergil, *Aeneid* I.513-14

8 *ellipsis* Omission of obvious words.

The apparition of these faces in the crowd;
Petals on a wet, black bough.   *Ezra Pound*

tum pius Aenēās: . . .
"Then dutiful Aeneas (said): . . . ."   Vergil, *Aeneid* V.26

9 *euphemism* Using a nice or pleasant expression to replace an unpleasant
one.

I shall whisper
Heavenly labials in a **world of gutturals**.   *Wallace Stevens*

[tellūs quae] et patris Anchīsae **gremiō complectitur ossa.**"
" '[The land that] also embraces the bones of my father Anchises in
her bosom.' "

Vergil, *Aeneid* V.30-31

10 *hendyadis* Using two connected nouns rather than a noun modified by an adjective or its equivalent ("two things meaning one").

> . . . humble-bee, Voyager of **light and noon**.   *Ralph Waldo Emerson*

> "quantās **aciēs strāgemque** ciēbunt!"
> " 'What great battles and destruction they will stir up!' "
> Vergil, *Aeneid* VI.829

10a *hypallage* Switching the relations between words.

> Speech without word and
> Word of no speech.   T. S. Eliot, *The Wasteland*

> **"dare classibus Austros."**
> "to give the south winds to the fleet (*instead of*
> to give the fleet to the south winds)"
> Vergil, *Aeneid* III.61

11 *hyperbole* Exaggeration.

> **They leaped the Mississippi, blue border of the West,**
> **From the Gulf to Canada, two thousand miles long.**
> *Vachel Lindsay*

> nec iam amplius ūllae
> appārent terrae, **caelum undique** et **undique pontus**.
> "Nor any longer
> was dry land visible, the sky (was) everywhere and the
> sea
> everywhere."
> Vergil, *Aeneid* III.192-93

12 *hysteron-proteron* Reversal of the common order.

> **"moriāmur** et **in media arma ruāmus!"**
> " 'Let us die and rush to arms!' "   Vergil, *Aeneid* II.353

13 *litotes* Affirming something by denying its opposite.

> There is **no end**, only addition.   *T. S. Eliot*

> "post mihi **nōn similī poenā** commissa luētis."
> " 'Hereafter, you will pay me back for your crimes with a much
> greater punishment [=with no similar punishment].' "
> Vergil, *Aeneid* I.136

14 *metaphor* Using a word to refer to something which is different from, but similar to it.

The world's an **orphans' home**.   *Marianne Moore*

iamque ferē **mediam caeli** Nox ūmida **mētam**
contigerat.
"And now dewy Night had almost reached the central turning-post
  of the sky."

Vergil, *Aeneid* V.835-36

15 *metonymy* Substituting a word for a related word, e.g. cause for effect, container for contained.

Freedom's young apostles . . .
All **chains** from limb and spirit strike.   *John Greenleaf Whittier*

"hīs ego nigrantem commixtā grandine **nimbum**

. . .
dēsuper īnfundam et tonitrū caelum omne ciēbō."
" 'On these, I will pour out from above a black cloud,
  with hail mixed in,
and I will roil the entire sky with my thunder.' "

Vergil, *Aeneid* IV.120-22

16 *onomatopoeia* A word or phrase that sounds like what it means.

"Boomlay, boomlay, Boom,"
While the witch-men laughed, with a sinister air,
And sang with the scalawags prancing there.

Vachel Lindsay, *The Congo*

rādit iter **liquidum celerē** neque commovet **ālās**.
"[A dove] glides on her liquid journey, and does not move her
  nimble wings."

Vergil, *Aeneid* V.217

17 *oxymoron* A seeming contradiction in terms.

[Hollywood, where]
Alice and **Cinderella** are **most real**.   *Karl Shapiro*

illī **dūra quiēs** oculōs et **ferreus** urget
somnus.
"Hard rest and iron sleep press down on his eyes."

Vergil, *Aeneid* XII.309-10

18   *personification* Describing inanimate things as though animate.

Lilacs in dooryards
Holding quiet conversations with an early moon.   *Amy Lowell*

[illa=nāvis] ad terram **fugit** et portū **sē condidit** altō.
"The ship escaped to land and hid herself in the deep harbor."
Vergil, *Aeneid* V.243

19   *pleonasm* Using superfluous words for good effect.

Love is not all: **it is not meat nor drink**
Nor slumber nor a roof against the rain;
Nor yet a floating spar to men that sink
And rise and sink and rise and sink again.   *Edna St. Vincent Millay*

[Dīdō] candentis vaccae **media inter cornua** fundit.
"[Dido] poured (wine) in the middle, between the horns of a white
    cow."
Vergil, *Aeneid* IV.61

20   *polysyndeton* Using several conjunctions for effect.

Outward **and** outward **and** forever outward.   *Walt Whitman*

laeva tenent Thetis **et** Melitē Panopaea**que** virgō,
Nīsaeē Spīō**que** Thalīa**que** Cȳmodocē**que**.
"Thetis and Melite and the virgin Panopaea dominate the left,
    (also) Nisaea and Spio and Thalia and Cymodoce."
Vergil, *Aeneid* V.825-26

21   *simile* An expressed comparison.

My soul is like the oar that momently
    Dies in a desperate stress beneath the wave,
Then glitters out again and sweeps the sea.   *Sidney Lanier*

ac ventī velut agmine factō,
quā data porta, ruunt et terrās turbine perflant.
        "And the winds, as if in a military line,
rush where there is a breach, and blow across the earth in a tornado."
Vergil, *Aeneid* I.82-83

22   *syncope* Loss of letters within a word.

"I**'d** not be in a hurry to say that."
"I have**n't** been."   *Robert Frost*

. . . nunc placidā **compostus** [=compositus] pāce quiēscit.
"Now [Teucer], settled, rests in gentle peace."
Vergil, *Aeneid* I.249

23 *synecdoche* Substituting a part for a whole.

> Here we must eat our **salt** or our **bones** starve.   *Archibald MacLeish*

> . . . flammās cum rēgia **puppis**
> extulerat.
> . . . "when the royal stern [= ship] had raised
> the signal-fires."
>
> Vergil, *Aeneid* II.256-57

24 *tmesis* Separating the two parts of a compound word.

> bis collō squāmea **circum**
> terga **datī** superant capite et cervīcibus altīs.
> "[The snakes] twisted their scaly backs around his neck twice, and
> overwhelmed him [=Laocoön] with their heads and steep necks."
>
> Vergil, *Aeneid* II.218-19

25 *zeugma* Using one verb (or adjective) to apply to two or more parallel
nouns or clauses.

> I passed the storm-racked gate
> Of Hudson Strait,
> **And savage Chidley** where the warring tides
> In white wrath seethe for ever.   *Sir Charles G. D. Roberts*

> nunc **hōs**, nunc **illōs aditūs**, omnemque pererrat
> arte locum.
> "He [=Dares] first this approach, now that, surveys
> the whole ground with dexterity."
>
> Vergil, *Aeneid* V.441-42

VOCABULARY

Listed below are words used in Latin exercises in Sections **1-30**.
They are listed in the ways described in Section **31**.

a

ā, ab + *abl. from; by*
abeō, abīre, abiī, abitum *go away*
accipiō, accipere, accēpī, acceptum *accept,*
receive
ad + *acc. to, at*
adeō *so much, so greatly*
adhūc *until now, still*
adipīscor, adipīscī, adeptus sum *receive,*
obtain
adiuvō, adiuvāre, adiūvī, adiūtum *help*
adstō, adstāre, adstitī *stand by*
adveniō, advenīre, advēnī, adventum *arrive*
aedificō, aedificāre, aedificāvī, aedificātum
build
aeger, aegra, aegrum *sick, ill*
Aegyptius, Aegyptia, Aegyptium *Egyptian*
afferō, afferre, attulī, adlātum (*sometimes*
allātum) *bring*
afflīgō, afflīgere, afflīxī, afflīctum *afflict,*
strike
ager, agrī, m. *field*
aggredior, aggredī, aggressus sum *attack*
agnus, agnī, m. *lamb*
agō, agere, ēgī, āctum *do, act*
grātiās agō *thank, give thanks*
agricola, agricolae, m. *farmer*
alius, alia, aliud *other, another*
aliī . . . aliī *some . . . others*
alter, altera, alterum *the other, another*
alter . . . alter *one . . . the other*
ambulō, ambulāre, ambulāvī, ambulātum
walk
amīcus, amīcī, m. *friend*
āmittō, āmittere, āmīsī, āmissum *lose*
amō, amāre, amāvī, amātum *love, like*
amphitheātrum, amphitheātrī, n.
amphitheater
an *or*
utrum . . . an *whether . . . or*
ancilla, ancillae, f. *slave-girl, slave-woman*
animal, animālis, n. *animal*
annus, annī, m. *year*

ante + *acc. before*
aperiō, aperīre, aperuī, apertum *open*
apodytērium, apodytēriī, n. *changing room*
appāreō, appārēre, appāruī, appāritum
appear
appropinquō, appropinquāre,
appropinquāvī, appropinquātum + *dat.*
approach, come near to
aqua, aquae, f. *water*
āra, ārae, f. *altar*
arcessō, arcessere, arcessīvī, arcessītum
summon, send for
ardeō, ardēre, arsī *burn, be on fire*
ars, artis, f. *art, skill*
Athēnae, Athēnārum, f.pl. *Athens*
āthlēta, āthlētae, m. *athlete*
atque *and*
attonitus, attonita, attonitum *astonished*
attulī *see* afferō
auctor, auctōris, m. *creator, originator*
audeō, audēre, ausus sum *dare*
audiō, audīre, audīvī, audītum *hear*
auferō, auferre, abstulī, ablātum *take away,*
steal
aula, aulae, f. *palace*
aurum, aurī, n. *gold*
autem *but*
auxilium, auxiliī, n. *help*
avārus, avārī, m. *miser*
avis, avis, f. *bird*

b

barba, barbae, f. *beard*
bellum, bellī, n. *war*
bellum gerere *wage war, campaign*
bene *well*
benignus, benigna, benignum *kind*
bibō, bibere, bibī *drink*
bis *twice*
bonus, bona, bonum *good*
Britannī, Britannōrum, m.pl. *Britons*
Britannia, Britanniae, f. *Britain*

c

caelum, caelī, n. *sky, heaven*
calidus, calida, calidum *hot*
callidus, callida, callidum *clever, smart*
candidātus, candidātī, m. *candidate*
canis, canis, m. *dog*
cantō, cantāre, cantāvī, cantātum *sing*
capiō, capere, cēpī, captum *take, catch, capture*
captīvus, captīvī, m. *prisoner, captive*
caput, capitis, n. *head*
carcer, carceris, m. *prison*
castra, castrōrum, n.pl. *camp*
catēna, catēnae, f. *chain*
caveō, cavēre, cāvī, cautum *beware*
celebrō, celebrāre, celebrāvī, celebrātum *celebrate*
celeriter *quickly, fast*
cēlō, cēlāre, cēlāvī, cēlātum *hide*
cēna, cēnae, f. *dinner*
centum *a hundred*
centuriō, centuriōnis, m. *centurion*
cēterī, cēterae, cētera *the others, the rest*
chorus, chorī, m. *chorus, choir*
cibus, cibī, m. *food*
circumspectō, circumspectāre, circumspectāvī, circumspectātum *look around*
circumveniō, circumvenīre, circumvēnī, circumventum *surround*
cīvis, cīvis, m.f. *citizen*
clāmō, clāmāre, clāmāvī, clāmātum *shout*
clāmor, clāmōris, m. *shout, uproar*
claudō, claudere, clausī, clausum *shut, close*
cliēns, clientis, m. *client*
cōgitō, cōgitāre, cōgitāvī, cōgitātum *think, consider*
cognōscō, cognōscere, cognōvī, cognitum *get to know, find out*
cōgō, cōgere, coēgī, coāctum *force, compel*
comitor, comitārī, comitātus sum *accompany*
comparō, comparāre, comparāvī, comparātum *obtain*
compleō, complēre, complēvī, complētum *fill*
conclāve, conclāvis, n. *room*
condūcō, condūcere, condūxī, conductum *hire*
cōnfīdō, cōnfīdere, cōnfīsus sum + dat.*trust, put trust*
cōnor, cōnārī, cōnātus sum *try*
cōnsilium, cōnsiliī, n. *plan, idea*

cōnsistō, cōnsistere, cōnstitī *stand firm, halt*
cōnspiciō, cōnspicere, cōnspexī, cōnspectum *catch sight of*
cōnspicor, cōnspicārī, cōnspicātus sum *catch sight of*
cōnsul, cōnsulis, m. *consul (senior magistrate)*
cōnsūmō, cōnsūmere, cōnsūmpsī, cōnsūmptum *eat, consume*
cōnsurgō, cōnsurgere, cōnsurrēxī, cōnsurrēctum *jump up*
contendō, contendere, contendī, contentum *hurry*
contentus, contenta, contentum *satisfied*
contrā + acc. *against*
coquus, coquī, m. *cook*
corpus, corporis, n. *body*
cotīdiē *every day*
crās *tomorrow*
crēdō, crēdere, crēdidī, crēditum + dat. *trust, believe*
crūdēlitās, crūdēlitātis, f. *cruelty*
cubiculum, cubiculī, n. *bedroom*
cuius *see* quī
cum *when*
cūr? *why?*
currō, currere, cucurrī, cursum *run*
custōs, custōdis, m. *guard*

d

dabam *see* dō
damnō, damnāre, damnāvī, damnātum *condemn*
damnōsus, damnōsa, damnōsum *fatal*
dē + abl. *from, down from; about, over*
dea, deae, f. *goddess*
dēbeō, dēbēre, dēbuī, dēbitum *ought, should, must*
decem *ten*
decet, decēre, decuit *is proper*
    mē decet *I ought*
dēcidō, dēcidere, dēcidī *fall down*
dēcipiō, dēcipere, dēcēpī, dēceptum *deceive, trick*
dēcurrō, dēcurrere, dēcurrī, dēcursum *run down, speed, race*
dedī *see* dō
deinde *then*
dēlectō, dēlectāre, dēlectāvī, dēlectātum *delight, please*
dēleō, dēlēre, dēlēvī, dēlētum *destroy*
dēnārius, dēnāriī, m. *denarius (a coin)*

dēns, dentis, m. *tooth*
dērīdeō, dērīdēre, dērīsī, dērīsum *mock, jeer at*
dēserō, dēserere, dēseruī, dēsertum *desert, leave behind*
dēsiliō, dēsilīre, dēsiluī, dēsultum *jump down*
dēsinō, dēsinere, dēsiī, dēsitum *end, cease*
dēspērō, dēspērāre, dēspērāvī, dēspērātum *despair, give up*
deus, deī, m. *god*
Dēva, Dēvae, f. *Chester (England)*
dīcō, dīcere, dīxī, dictum *say*
dictō, dictāre, dictāvī, dictātum *dictate*
diēs, diēī, m. f. *day*
    diēs nātālis, diēī nātālis, m. *birthday*
difficilis, difficile *difficult*
dignus, digna, dignum + abl. *worthy*
dīligenter *carefully*
discēdō, discēdere, discessī, discessum *depart*
discō, discere, didicī *learn*
discus, discī, m. *discus*
diū *for a long time*
dīves, gen. dīvitis *rich*
dīvitiae, dīvitiārum, f.pl. *riches*
dō, dare, dedī, datum *give*
doceō, docēre, docuī, doctum *teach*
domina, dominae, f. *mistress*
dominus, dominī, m. *master*
domus, domūs, f. *home, house*
dōnec *until*
dōnō, dōnāre, dōnāvī, dōnātum *give*
dōnum, dōnī, n. *present, gift*
dormiō, dormīre, dormīvī, dormītum *sleep*
dūcō, dūcere, dūxī, ductum *lead*
dum *while*
duo, duae, duo *two*
dūrus, dūra, dūrum *hard*
dux, ducis, m. *leader*

e

ē, ex + abl. *from, out of*
eam *see* is
eandem *see* īdem
eās *see* is
ecce! *see! look!*
efficiō, efficere, effēcī, effectum *carry out, accomplish*
effugiō, effugere, effūgī *escape*
effundō, effundere, effūdī, effūsum *pour out*

ēgī *see* agō
ego, meī *I, me*
ēgredior, ēgredī, ēgressus sum *go out*
ēheu! *alas!*
eī *see* is
eīdem *see* īdem
eīs *see* is
elephantus, elephantī, m. *elephant*
ēligō, ēligere, ēlēgī, ēlēctum *choose*
emō, emere, ēmī, ēmptum *buy*
eō, īre, iī, itum *go*
    obviam eō *meet, go to meet*
eōdem *see* īdem
epistula, epistulae, f. *letter*
eques, equitis, m. *horseman*
equus, equī, m. *horse*
eram *see* sum
ēripiō, ēripere, ēripuī, ēreptum *snatch away*
erō *see* sum
ērudiō, ērudīre, ērudiī, ērudītum *teach*
es, est *see* sum
et *and*
etiam *even, also*
eum *see* is
ex, ē + abl. *from, out of*
excitō, excitāre, excitāvī, excitātum *arouse, wake up, awaken*
exclāmō, exclāmāre, exclāmāvī, exclāmātum *exclaim, shout*
exeō, exīre, exiī, exitum *go out*
exerceō, exercēre, exercuī, exercitum *exercise, practice, train*
exigō, exigere, exēgī, exāctum *demand*
exiguus, exigua, exiguum *small, short*
exspectō, exspectāre, exspectāvī, exspectātum *wait for*
exstinguō, exstinguere, exstīnxī, exstīnctum *extinguish, put out*
extrā + acc. *outside*
extrahō, extrahere, extrāxī, extractum *pull out*

f

faber, fabrī, m. *craftsman*
facile *easily*
facilis, facile *easy*
faciō, facere, fēcī, factum *make, do*
    iter faciō *make a journey, travel*
    rebelliōnem faciō *rebel*
falsus, falsa, falsum *false, untrue*

133

faveō, favēre, fāvī, fautum + *dat. favor,
    support*
fēmina, fēminae, f. *woman*
fenestra, fenestrae, f. *window*
ferō, ferre, tulī, lātum *bring, carry*
fervidus, fervida, fervidum *intense, fierce*
fessus, fessa, fessum *tired*
festīnō, festīnāre, festīnāvī, festīnātum
    hurry
fidēliter *faithfully*
fidēs, fideī, f. *faith*
fīlius, fīliī, m. *son*
fīō, fierī, factus sum *be made, be done, become*
flamma, flammae, f. *flame*
flētus, flētūs, m. *weeping, tears*
flūmen, flūminis, n. *river*
foedus, foeda, foedum *foul, horrible*
fortis, forte *brave*
forum, forī, n. *forum, market-place*
fossa, fossae, f. *ditch*
frangō, frangere, frēgī, frāctum *break*
frāter, frātris, m. *brother*
fraus, fraudis, f. *trick*
frūmentum, frūmentī, n. *grain*
frūstrā *in vain*
fugiō, fugere, fūgī, fugitum *run away, flee
    (from)*
fuī *see* sum
fundus, fundī, m. *farm*
fūr, fūris, m. *thief*

g
Gallia, Galliae, f. *Gaul*
gaudeō, gaudēre, gāvīsus sum *be pleased,
    rejoice, be delighted*
gemma, gemmae, f. *jewel, gem*
gener, generī, m. *son-in-law*
gerō, gerere, gessī, gestum *achieve*
  bellum gerō *wage war, campaign*
gladiātor, gladiātōris, m. *gladiator*
gladius, gladiī, m. *sword*
glōria, glōriae, f. *glory*
gracilis, gracile *slender, slim*
gradior, gradī, gressus sum *go*
Graecus, Graeca, Graecum *Greek*
grātiae, grātiārum, f.pl. *thanks*
  grātiās agō *thank, give thanks*
gustō, gustāre, gustāvī, gustātum *taste*

h
habeō, habēre, habuī, habitum *have*
habitō, habitāre, habitāvī, habitātum *live*
haereō, haerēre, haesī, haesum *stick, cling*
haesitō, haesitāre, haesitāvī, haesitātum
    hesitate
haruspex, haruspicis, m. *soothsayer, diviner*
hasta, hastae, f. *spear*
heri *yesterday*
hic, haec, hoc *this*
Hispānia, Hispāniae, f. *Spain*
hodiē *today*
homō, hominis, m. *man*
hōra, hōrae, f. *hour*
horreum, horreī, n. *barn, granary*
hortor, hortārī, hortātus sum *encourage, urge*
hortus, hortī, m. *garden*
hospes, hospitis, m. *guest*
hostis, hostis, m.f. *enemy*
humilis, humile *low-born, of low class*

i
iaciō, iacere, iēcī, iactum *throw*
iam *now*
iānua, iānuae, f. *door*
ībō *see* eō
id *see* is
īdem, eadem, idem *(for endings, see* 5.6*) the
    same*
ignōscō, ignōscere, ignōvī, ignōtum + *dat.
    forgive*
ille, illa, illud *that*
immemor, *gen.* immemoris + *gen. forgetful*
impediō, impedīre, impedīvī, impedītum
    delay, hinder
imperātor, imperātōris, m. *emperor*
imperō, imperāre, imperāvī, imperātum +
    dat. order, command
in (1) + *acc. into, onto*
in (2) + *abl. in, on*
incendō, incendere, incendī, incēnsum
    burn, set fire to
incertus, incerta, incertum *uncertain*
induō, induere, induī, indūtum *put on*
īnfēlīx, *gen.* īnfēlīcis *unlucky*
īnferō, īnferre, intulī, inlātum *(sometimes
    illātum) bring in*
ingēns, *gen.* ingentis *huge*
ingredior, ingredī, ingressus sum *enter*
inimīcus, inimīcī, m. *enemy*
innocēns, *gen.* innocentis *innocent*

inquit *says, said*

īnsānus, īnsāna, īnsānum *crazy, insane*

īnspiciō, īnspicere, īnspexī, īnspectum *look at, examine*

īnstruō, īnstruere, īnstrūxī, īnstrūctum *draw up*

interficiō, interficere, interfēcī, interfectum *kill*

intrō, intrāre, intrāvī, intrātum *enter*

intulī *see* īnferō

inveniō, invenīre, invēnī, inventum *find*

invītō, invītāre, invītāvī, invītātum *invite*

ipse, ipsa, ipsum *himself, herself, itself*

īrātus, īrāta, īrātum *angry*

is, ea, id (*for endings, see* 5.5) *he, she, it*

id quod *what*

ita *in this way, so*

Ītalia, Ītaliae, f. *Italy*

iter, itineris, n. *journey*

iter faciō *make a journey, travel*

iterum *again*

iubeō, iubēre, iussī, iussum *order*

iūdex, iūdicis, m. *judge*

iuvenis, iuvenis, m. *young man*

l

labōrō, labōrāre, labōrāvī, labōrātum *work*

lacrimō, lacrimāre, lacrimāvī, lacrimātum *weep, cry*

lapis, lapidis, m. *stone*

latrō, latrōnis, m. *robber*

lātus *see* ferō

lātus, lāta, lātum *wide*

laudō, laudāre, laudāvī, laudātum *praise*

laus, laudis, f. *praise, fame*

lavō, lavāre, lāvī, lautum *wash*

lectus, lectī, m. *couch, bed*

lēgātus, lēgātī, m. *commander*

legō, legere, lēgī, lēctum *read*

leō, leōnis, m. *lion*

libellus, libellī, m. *little book*

liber, librī, m. *book*

līberō, līberāre, līberāvī, līberātum *free, set free*

lībertās, lībertātis, f. *freedom*

libet, libēre, libuit, libitum *is pleasing*

mihi libet *I am glad*

licet, licēre, licuit, licitum *is allowed*

mē licet *I may*

līmen, līminis, n. *threshold, doorway*

locus, locī, m. *place*

Londinium, Londiniī, n. *London*

loquor, loquī, locūtus sum *speak*

lūdō, lūdere, lūsī, lūsum *play*

lupus, lupī, m. *wolf*

lūx, lūcis, f. *light, daylight*

prīmā lūce *at dawn*

lyricus, lyrica, lyricum *lyric*

m

magister, magistrī, m. *master, teacher*

magnus, magna, magnum *big, large, great*

maximus, maxima, maximum *very big, very great, greatest*

malus, mala, malum *evil, bad*

pessimus, pessima, pessimum *very bad, worst*

māne *in the morning*

maneō, manēre, mānsī, mānsum *remain, stay*

mare, maris, n. *sea*

marītus, marītī, m. *husband*

māter, mātris, f. *mother*

maximus *see* magnus

mē *see* ego

medicus, medicī, m. *doctor*

medius, media, medium *middle, (in) the middle of*

membrum, membrī, n. *limb*

meminī, meminisse *remember*

mendāx, mendācis, m. *liar*

mēnsa, mēnsae, f. *table*

mēnsis, mēnsis, m. *month*

mentior, mentīrī, mentītus sum *lie, tell a lie*

mercātor, mercātōris, m. *merchant*

mereō, merēre, meruī, meritum *deserve*

meus, mea, meum *my, mine*

mihi *see* ego

mīles, mīlitis, m. *soldier*

mīlitō, mīlitāre, mīlitāvī, mīlitātum *be a soldier*

minus *less*

mīrābilis, mīrābile *marvelous, strange, wonderful*

mīror, mīrārī, mīrātus sum *admire, wonder at*

miser, misera, miserum *miserable, wretched, sad*

mittō, mittere, mīsī, missum *send*

modus, modī, m. *manner, way, kind*

quō modō? *how? in what way?*

moneō, monēre, monuī, monitum *warn, advise*

mōns, montis, m. *mountain*

morbus, morbī, m. *illness*

morior, morī, mortuus sum *die*

  moritūrus, moritūra, moritūrum *about to die, going to die*

  mortuus, mortua, mortuum *dead*

moror, morārī, morātus sum *delay, hold steady*

mox *soon*

multus, multa, multum *much*

  multō *(by) much*

mūrus, mūrī, m. *wall*

n

nam *for*

nārrō, nārrāre, nārrāvī, nārrātum *tell, relate*

(diēs) nātālis, (diēī) nātālis, m. *birthday*

nātus, nātī, m. *son*

nauta, nautae, m. *sailor*

nāvis, nāvis, f. *ship*

-ne *asks a question*

nē *that . . . not, so that . . . not, in order that . . . not*

nec *and not, nor*

necō, necāre, necāvī, necātum *kill*

negō, negāre, negāvī, negātum *deny, say that . . . not*

nēmō *no one, nobody*

nescio, nescīre, nescīvī, nescītum *not know*

nihil *nothing*

nimis *too much, too*

nisi *except, unless, if . . . not*

noceō, nocēre, nocuī, nocitum + *dat. hurt*

nōlō, nōlle, nōluī *not want, refuse*

  nōlī, nōlīte *do not, don't*

nōmen, nōminis, n. *name*

nōn *not*

nōnne? *surely?*

nōs *we, us*

noster, nostra, nostrum *our*

novus, nova, novum *new*

nox, noctis, f. *night*

nūllus, nūlla, nūllum *not any, no*

num? *surely . . . not?*

numerō, numerāre, numerāvī, numerātum *count*

nunc *now*

nūntiō, nūntiāre, nūntiāvī, nūntiātum *announce*

nūntius, nūntiī, m. *messenger*

o

obscēnus, obscēna, obscēnum *rude, obscene*

obscūrus, obscūra, obscūrum *dark, gloomy*

obtineō, obtinēre, obtinuī, obtentum *occupy*

obviam eō, obviam īre, obviam iī, obviam itum + *dat. meet, go to meet*

occāsiō, occāsiōnis, f. *opportunity*

occīdō, occīdere, occīdī, occīsum *kill*

occupō, occupāre, occupāvī, occupātum *seize, take over*

octō *eight*

ōdī, ōdisse *hate, dislike*

odium, odiī, n. *hatred*

  odiō sum *be hateful*

offerō, offerre, obtulī, oblātum *offer*

ōmen, ōminis, n. *omen*

omnis, omne *all, every*

  omnia *all, everything*

opera, operae, f. *work, attention*

oportet, oportēre, oportuit *is right*

  mē oportet *I must*

oppidum, oppidī, n. *town*

opprimō, opprimere, oppressī, oppressum *crush*

ōs, ōris, n. *mouth, face*

p

paenitet, paenitēre, paenituit *be sorry, regret*

  mē paenitet *I regret, I am sorry*

parcō, parcere, pepercī, parsum + *dat. spare*

parēns, parentis, m.f. *parent*

pāreō, pārēre, pāruī, pāritum + *dat. obey*

pāstor, pāstōris, m. *shepherd*

pater, patris, m. *father*

patior, patī, passus sum *suffer, endure, allow*

pauper, *gen.* pauperis *poor*

pecūnia, pecūniae, f. *money*

pelagus, pelagī, n. *sea*

pepercī *see* parcō

per + *acc. through, along*

pereō, perīre, periī, peritum *die, perish*

perficiō, perficere, perfēcī, perfectum *finish*

perīculōsus, perīculōsa, perīculōsum *dangerous*

perīculum, perīculī, n. *danger*

persuādeō, persuādēre, persuāsī, persuāsum + *dat. persuade*

perterritus, perterrita, perterritum *terrified*

perveniō, pervenīre, pervēnī, perventum *reach, arrive at*

pessimus *see* malus

petō, petere, petīvī, petītum *head for; seek,
    beg for, ask for*
pictūra, pictūrae, f. *picture*
piscis, piscis, m. *fish*
placeō, placēre, placuī, placitum + *dat.*
    please, suit
plaudō, plaudere, plausī, plausum + *dat.*
    applaud, clap
pluit, pluere, pluit *rain*
poēta, poētae, m. *poet*
polliceor, pollicērī, pollicitus sum *promise*
pompa, pompae, f. *procession*
Pompēiī, Pompēiōrum, m.pl. *Pompeii*
pōnō, pōnere, posuī, positum *put, place*
pōns, pontis, m. *bridge*
populus, populī, m. *people*
porcus, porcī, m. *pig*
porta, portae, f. *gate*
portō, portāre, portāvī, portātum *carry*
portus, portūs, m. *harbor*
possum, posse, potuī *can, be able*
postquam *after, when*
postulō, postulāre, postulāvī, postulātum
    demand
praecō, praecōnis, m. *herald*
praemium, praemiī, n. *prize, reward*
praesum, praeesse, praefuī + *dat. be in
    charge of*
praetereō, praeterīre, praeteriī, praeteritum
    pass by, go past
precor, precārī, precātus sum *pray*
pretiōsus, pretiōsa, pretiōsum *expensive,
    precious*
prīmus, prīma, prīmum *first*
    prīmā lūce *at dawn*
prīncipia, prīncipiōrum, n.pl. *headquarters*
priusquam *before*
prōcēdō, prōcēdere, prōcessī, prōcessum
    advance, proceed
prōcurrō, prōcurrere, prōcurrī, prōcursum
    project
proficīscor, proficīscī, profectus sum *set out*
prōgredior, prōgredī, prōgressus sum
    advance
prohibeō, prohibēre, prohibuī, prohibitum
    prevent
prōmittō, prōmittere, prōmīsī, prōmissum
    promise
prōnus, prōna, prōnum *easy*
prope + *acc. near*
prūdēns, *gen.* prūdentis *shrewd, sensible*

pudet, pudēre, puduit, puditum *be ashamed*
    mē pudet *I am ashamed*
puella, puellae, f. *girl, girlfriend*
puer, puerī, m. *boy*
pugna, pugnae, f. *fight*
pugnō, pugnāre, pugnāvī, pugnātum *fight*
pūniō, pūnīre, pūnīvī, pūnītum *punish*
puto, putāre, putāvī, putātum *think*

q
quā? *see* quī?
quam *how*
    tam . . . quam *as . . . as*
quamquam *although*
quamvīs *although*
quandō? *when?*
quārē? *why?*
quasi *as if*
-que *and*
    -que . . . -que *both . . . and*
quī, quae, quod (*for endings, see 5.7*) *who,
    which*
    id quod *what*
quī? quae? quod? *which? what?*
quia *because*
quīdam, quaedam, quoddam *one, a certain*
quīntus, quīnta, quīntum *fifth*
quis? quid? *who? what?*
quō modō? *how? in what way?*
quod *because*
quot? *how many?*

r
rapiō, rapere, rapuī, raptum *seize, grab*
rebelliō, rebelliōnis, f. *rebellion, uprising*
    rebelliōnem faciō *rebel*
recipiō, recipere, recēpī, receptum *recover,
    take back*
recitō, recitāre, recitāvī, recitātum *recite, read
    out*
recūsō, recūsāre, recūsāvī, recūsātum *refuse*
reddō, reddere, reddidī, redditum *give back*
redeō, redīre, rediī, reditum *return, go back,
    come back*
redūcō, redūcere, redūxī, reductum *lead back*
reficiō, reficere, refēcī, refectum *repair*
rēgīna, rēgīnae, f. *queen*
regiō, regiōnis, f. *region*
regredior, regredī, regressus sum *go back,
    return*
relinquō, relinquere, relīquī, relictum *leave*

requīrō, requīrere, requīsīvī, requīsītum
   ask, seek, search for
rēs, reī, f. *thing, business*
resistō, resistere, restitī + *dat. resist*
respondeō, respondēre, respondī,
   respōnsum *reply*
retineō, retinēre, retinuī, retentum *keep,
   restrain*
reveniō, revenīre, revēnī, reventum *come
   back, return*
rēx, rēgis, m. *king*
rīdeō, rīdēre, rīsī, rīsum *laugh, smile*
rīpa, rīpae, f. *river bank*
rogō, rogāre, rogāvī, rogātum *ask*
Rōma, Rōmae, f. *Rome*
Rōmānī, Rōmānōrum, m.pl. *Romans*
ruō, ruere, ruī *rush*
rūs, rūris, n. *country, countryside*

s

sacerdōs, sacerdōtis, m. *priest*
sacrificō, sacrificāre, sacrificāvī, sacrificātum
   sacrifice
saepe *often*
saeviō, saevīre, saeviī, saevītum *be in a rage*
saevus, saeva, saevum *savage, cruel*
salūtō, salūtāre, salūtāvī, salūtātum *greet,
   hail*
satis *enough*
saxum, saxī, n. *rock*
scelestus, scelesta, scelestum *wicked*
scelus, sceleris, n. *crime*
scindō, scindere, scidī, scissum *tear, cut*
scio, scīre, scīvī, scītum *know*
scrībō, scrībere, scrīpsī, scrīptum *write*
sē *himself, herself, themselves*
   (*for se used in indirect statements, see* 25.4d)
secundus, secunda, secundum *second*
sedeō, sedēre, sēdī, sessum *sit*
semper *always*
senātor, senātōris, m. *senator*
senex, senis, m. *old man*
septem *seven*
sequor, sequī, secūtus sum *follow*
serviō, servīre, servīvī, servītum + *dat. serve*
   (*as a slave)*
servō, servāre, servāvī, servātum *save, look
   after*
servus, servī, m. *slave*
sevērē *severely*
sexāgintā *sixty*

sextus, sexta, sextum *sixth*
sī *if*
Sicilia, Siciliae, f. *Sicily*
sīcut *like*
signum, signī, n. *sign, signal*
silva, silvae, f. *wood*
sim *see* sum
similis, simile + *dat. similar*
simulac, simulatque *as soon as*
soleō, solēre, solitus sum *be accustomed*
sollicitus, sollicita, sollicitum *worried, anxious*
sōlus, sōla, sōlum *alone, only*
sonō, sonāre, sonuī, sonitum *sound*
soror, sorōris, f. *sister*
spectātor, spectātōris, m. *spectator*
spectō, spectāre, spectāvī, spectātum *look at,
   watch*
spērō, spērāre, spērāvī, spērātum *hope,
   expect*
statim *at once*
statua, statuae, f. *statue*
stō, stāre, stetī, statum *stand*
strepitus, strepitūs, m. *noise, din*
stultus, stulta, stultum *stupid, foolish*
suāviter *sweetly*
sub + *abl. under, beneath*
subitō *suddenly*
sum, esse, fuī *be*
summus, summa, summum *highest, greatest*
superbē *arrogantly, proudly*
superō, superāre, superāvī, superātum
   overcome, surpass
supplicium, suppliciī, n. *punishment, penalty*
surgō, surgere, surrēxī, surrēctum *get up,
   rise*
suspicor, suspicārī, suspicātus sum *suspect*
suus, sua, suum *his, her, their*

t

taberna, tabernae, f. *shop, inn*
taceō, tacēre, tacuī, tacitum *be silent, be quiet*
tacitus, tacita, tacitum *quiet, silent, in silence*
tam *so*
   tam . . . quam *as . . . as*
tamen *however*
tandem *at last*
tangō, tangere, tetigī, tāctum *touch*
tantus, tanta, tantum *so great, such a great*
tardus, tarda, tardum *late, slow*
taurus, taurī, m. *bull*
tē *see* tū *you*

tempestās, tempestātis, f. *storm*
templum, templī, n. *temple*
temptō, temptāre, temptāvī, temptātum *try,*
    put to the test
tempus, temporis, n. *time*
terribilis, terribile *terrible*
testis, testis, m.f. *witness*
theātrum, theātrī, n. *theater*
tibi *see* tū
timeō, timēre, timuī *be afraid, fear*
tot *so many*
tōtus, tōta, tōtum *whole*
trādō, trādere, trādidī, trāditum *hand over*
trahō, trahere, trāxī, tractum *drag, draw*
trānseō, trānsīre, trānsiī, trānsitum *cross*
trēs, tria *three*
tū, tuī *you (singular)*
tuba, tubae, f. *trumpet*
tulī *see* ferō
tūtus, tūta, tūtum *safe*
tuus, tua, tuum *your (singular), yours*

u

ubi *where, when*
ultimus, ultima, ultimum *last*
umbra, umbrae, f. *shadow, ghost*
umquam *ever*
unda, undae, f. *wave*
undique *on all sides*
urbs, urbis, f. *city*
ut *(1) as*
ut *(2) that, so that, in order that*
utinam *if only, I wish that*
ūtor, ūtī, ūsus sum + *abl. use*
utrum *whether*
    utrum . . . an *whether . . . or*

v

valdē *very much, very*
vehementer *violently, loudly*
vehō, vehere, vexī, vectum *carry*
vellem *see* volō
vēndō, vēndere, vēndidī, vēnditum *sell*
venēnum, venēnī, n. *poison*
venia, veniae, f. *mercy*
veniō, venīre, vēnī, ventum *come*
verbum, verbī, n. *word*
vereor, verērī, veritus sum *be afraid, fear*
vērum, vērī, n. *truth*
vester, vestra, vestrum *your (plural)*
vestīmenta, vestīmentōrum, n.pl. *clothes*

vetō, vetāre, vetuī, vetitum *forbid*
vetus, *gen.* veteris *old*
vexō, vexāre, vexāvī, vexātum *annoy*
via, viae, f. *street*
victima, victimae, f. *victim*
victor, victōris, m. *victor, winner*
videō, vidēre, vīdī, vīsum *see*
vīlla, vīllae, f. *country-house, villa*
vinciō, vincīre, vīnxī, vīnctum *bind, tie up*
vincō, vincere, vīcī, victum *conquer, win, be*
    victorious
vīnum, vīnī, n. *wine*
vir, virī, m. *man*
virgō, virginis, f. *virgin*
vīs *see* volō *(want)*
vīsitō, vīsitāre, vīsitāvī, vīsitātum *visit*
vīta, vītae, f. *life*
vītō, vītāre, vītāvī, vītātum *avoid*
vituperō, vituperāre, vituperāvī,
    vituperātum *blame, curse*
vīvō, vīvere, vīxī, victum *live*
vocō, vocāre, vocāvī, vocātum *call*
volō, velle, voluī *want*
volō, volāre, volāvī, volātum *fly*
vōs *you (plural)*
vulnerō, vulnerāre, vulnerāvī, vulnerātum
    wound, injure
vulnus, vulneris, n. *wound*

INDEX

In this index, the bold numbers refer to Sections, followed by paragraph numbers. So, for example, the Accusative of time will be found in Section **14**, paragraph 5b, and Section **15**, paragraph 1a.